Wendy Grant has had an extremely varied career including engineering, teaching, parenting a large family, working with animals and managing a family business. She is qualified as a member of the Academy of Applied Psychology and The National Association of Hypnotists and Psychotherapists, and was accepted as an accredited member of the Hypnotherapy Register in 1993.

by the same author

Are You in Control?

WENDY GRANT

dare!

A BOOK FOR THOSE WHO
DARE TO CHANGE THEIR LIVES

ELEMENT
Shaftesbury, Dorset ● Rockport, Massachusetts
Brisbane, Queensland

First published by Eastbrook Publishing in 1993

This edition published in Great Britain in 1996 by
Element Books Limited
Shaftesbury, Dorset SP7 8BP

Published in the USA in 1996 by
Element Books, Inc.
PO Box 830, Rockport, MA 01966

Published in Australia in 1996 by
Element Books Limited
for Jacaranda Wiley Limited
33 Park Road, Milton, Brisbane 4064

Cover design by Max Fairbrother
Illustrations by Tony Thornhill
Design by Roger Lightfoot
Typeset by WestKey Ltd, Falmouth, Cornwall
Printed and bound in Great Britain by
BPC Paperbacks Ltd., Aylesbury

British Library Cataloguing-in-Publication
data available

Library of Congress Cataloging-in-Publication
data available

ISBN 1–85230–790–0

Contents

- Do you know how to make things happen in your life?
- Have you ever wished you were different?
- Have you longed to dare to be yourself?
- Are you too afraid of upsetting people to tell the truth?
- Do you dare to love – to express your emotions?
- Do you wish you could set yourself free from limitations?
- Do you dare to succeed – to be *really* successful?
- Do you dare to face your fears?
- Do you wish you dare have fun and be outrageous sometimes?
- Do you know how to be creative?
- Do you dread growing old and wish you dare to stay young?
- Would you like to realize your dreams?
- Do you wish you were more adventurous?
- Can you make decisions?
- Do you dare to let go of past conditioning and do things your way?
- Do you want to be happy?

This book will help set you free and take your *dares* and turn them into a reality.

Acknowledgements

I wish to acknowledge with gratitude the help and guidance given to me by Tom Gregory in writing and preparing this manuscript for publication. Also my thanks to Lyn Avery and Eric Fawcett for reading the script – I liked the funny comments too!

To my children: Simon, Steve, Tim, Patch, Sally and Jon.
And my grandchildren: Sam, Jack, William, Lydia, Rebbeca,
Jean-François and George.
This book could not have been written without all that I
have learnt from you.

Introduction

After several years of working as a therapist helping people to resolve emotional and behavioural problems, I was invited to lecture on the subject of the unconscious mind. This soon turned into a series of mini-workshops where my students learned to use self-hypnosis and visual techniques to make changes and take control of their own lives.

The next logical step seemed to be to write a book on the subject. And so I did. *Are You in Control?* is a step-by-step handbook designed to help those people who want to stop feeling as if they are being pushed around by life and enable them to control their own destiny. Past clients, students, and those who read the book were then asking me, 'What now? Where do I go next?' They wanted to know more. As I had been responsible for opening the door to their personal awareness and spiritual growth, they were turning to me for guidance. I realized that you can't help someone climb half-way up a mountain and then abandon them.

'I wish I dared to be myself' or 'If only I dared to be different' was uttered so often during consultancy sessions and in class that it seemed the time had come to write my next book – one showing people how to take the 'dare' and turn it into a reality.

Daring to let go of our defences needs insight and courage. When we remove fear, when we refuse to submit to it, we set ourselves free.

Wishing, however, is not enough. You may want to be different, successful, express yourself freely, be creative or original, but in doing so you don't want to upset or hurt people. Perhaps you find it hard to take the ridicule or denial that may follow any major change you make; you may believe that special ingredients are necessary for success; you may think that you require special talents or gifts to be different or change direction.

We cannot, and must not allow other people – whatever they may think or say about us – to control our lives or shape our destiny; neither can we hold them responsible for the results.

This is not a book about how to be blatantly selfish. It is a guide along the path to expressing yourself honestly – to help you attain a higher level of being.

Your life is precious, wonderful, unique, and it belongs to you. How you present yourself to the world, the way in which you handle your life, and whether it holds meaning and purpose, is not a matter of luck or misfortune, it is up to you. If another human being can do a thing, then it is also possible for you to achieve a similar goal.

In the following pages I have endeavoured to bring together thoughts, ideas, experiences and techniques that can be absorbed, learned and used by *those who dare*.

Wendy Grant

Note: Where case histories, stories and examples have been used, names, location and personal details have been changed to protect the confidentiality of those people.

1

Making Things Happen

In order to benefit from this book I am going to ask you first to do a little exercise with your imagination. By the end of the book I hope that you will be doing this for real! You need to realize from the beginning that no one can change your life for you, but reading through this book and doing the exercises will enable you to change your own life in whatever way you choose.

For the next few minutes let's just imagine that you are set free from all the limitations that have been preventing you from being your true self and from doing those things you would like to be able to do with your life. I want you to get a feel of what it will be like to be the way you wish you dare to be.

Taking your time, read through the following exercise a couple of times, then close your eyes, and in a quiet, leisurely way, follow the instructions, replacing my suggestions for change, with those of your own.

Exercise One – Dumping Those Things That Have Held You Back

You may wish to make a tape recording of this exercise and then simply relax and follow the instructions. You can, if you choose, ask a trusted friend to read slowly the exercise for you as you relax and respond.

1 Make yourself comfortable, close your eyes and breath deeply. Relax. For a few minutes concentrate on your breathing. Let everything slow down. Now mentally check over your body, starting with your toes and feet. Think about each toe in turn, first on one foot and then on the other. As you begin to relax, one of the first things that you will become aware of is that you can barely feel some of your toes at all and you can no longer distinguish one toe from the next. Let your leg muscles relax . . . your calf muscles and your thigh muscles. Be aware of a feeling of heaviness in your legs as you let go and relax. Let your tummy muscles relax. Concentrate once more on your breathing. You will notice that your breathing pattern has changed, it has slowed down. As you sink deeper and deeper into the surface supporting you, feel the gentle pressure behind your back, beneath your bottom and the backs of your thighs. Now let all of those tiny muscles in your scalp relax. Allow a calm peaceful expression to spread across your face. You can feel your eyelids resting gently against your eyes and you let your eyelids feel so heavy, so comfortable and so relaxed. You are now ready to relax all of those muscles in your neck and shoulders. Imagine all the stress and tension from your head, neck and shoulders, flowing down through your arms and out through the tips of your fingers. Let yourself feel so heavy, so comfortable and so relaxed that you feel you just don't want

to move. Finally, notice the feelings and sensations in your hands and fingers. Pay attention to any tingling or throbbing, any warmth or coldness. Enjoy the feelings of total relaxation.

2 Now imagine you are walking down a road in a town – this can be one that is already familiar to you or one created by your imagination. It's a perfect kind of day and you are feeling relaxed and at peace with yourself. Maybe there are trees lining the road and you can hear birds chirping. It is a quiet road with only the occasional car passing by. Take time to create this scene, making it as real as possible.

3 As you walk, you begin to imagine how it would feel if you were free of all the limitations in your life. Some of these are set by yourself and others will have been placed upon you by other people. Think about being freed from them as you walk in the sunshine. Wouldn't it be lovely *not* to feel compelled to visit certain people who make you feel uncomfortable? Wouldn't it feel good to be able to say '*no*' to some of the family or friends sometimes? Wouldn't it be fantastic not to feel that you always have to try and keep the peace at home or at work? How would it feel to dress and look the way you want without being restrained by convention? Imagine speaking out in front of others without fear of ridicule, embarrassment or feelings of self-consciousness? And how would it feel to be really successful?

4 After walking and thinking about these things for a while you reach a large green rubbish bin on the side of the pavement. Here you pause, open the lid, and drop into it all those things that have been holding you back and preventing you from being the person you want to be. Name them to yourself one by one as you dump them in the bin. If you like, you could, in your imagination,

take a note pad and list them all before getting rid of them. Enjoy this experience. Remember to do it in a relaxed casual way. Those feelings you no longer want, you dump. It's as simple as that.

5 When you have completed this, or gone as far as you feel you want to at this moment in your life, continue on your way. Presently you find a bench where you can sit down in the gentle warmth of the sun and experience how good it feels to be free from those negative feelings.

6 Now take a few minutes to let your imagination run riot. How does it feel to be a success, or rich, or able to speak the truth? Imagine not being bothered by what other people think or say about you?

7 Set your first goal. Choose one area you are determined to change. Speak quietly to your unconscious mind and

Drop into the bin all those things that have been holding you back.

ask it to help you make those changes that are necessary.

8 Stay still for a few minutes longer and enjoy the feelings of total relaxation as you picture yourself sitting on that bench in the sun.

Note: Repeat this exercise each night over the next two weeks as you go to sleep. Where you have taken positive action, allow yourself to think about this and enjoy the beginnings of a new independence.

If you find it easy to use your imagination, this should have been a good experience for you. If you had problems – don't worry – you will work your way through them as you read this book.

Some of the responses you were getting probably made you feel a little anxious; you may have found that there were some things that you weren't ready yet to let go of; there may have been feelings of guilt, disloyalty, fear. They are all part of what you are going to learn to understand and to explore. What is important is that you at least start off by giving yourself a chance. The character you have been portraying in your life may have become so ingrained that it feels almost impossible to even imagine another way of living. However, the fact that you are reading this book tells you that you have a longing, a real desire in some way, or ways, to change and to be different. You will find that even making a small change at first can improve the quality of your life

Desire

Desire is the first ingredient to change. No matter what lip-service you may give to your dreams and wishing to be different, if there is no *real desire* you will never get beyond the first rung of the ladder.

Sometimes desire is no more than vague wishful thinking that something in your life, or the way you conduct yourself, will change. That isn't enough. It is up to you to make these things happen.

Having just used your imagination to picture change, and if you allowed yourself to experience the feelings resulting from that imagined change, then already you will have fired your desire. You will feel a want, a longing for things to be different.

All change is possible. It is possible for you. If you can think it, then you can make it happen. Every invention, every new path, every new concept, every new response, started as a thought.

To dare to be yourself you have to nurture the seeds of desire. Wanting without conviction only adds to a sense of hopelessness and can become very depressing.

Many people feel they have no right, or that they do not deserve what they see other people enjoying freely. The truth is that if another has that right, then so do you.

Then there are those who believe that there is not sufficient for them to have a slice of the cake, that top positions, certain jobs, money and recognition are all rationed. They are not! The only limitations are those made within the mind.

If someone else wins the pools – some ordinary kind of person like you – then that should instil hope and optimism in you; it tells you that you too can have the good things in life.

I recently read somewhere that 'Success is mainly due to luck – ask any failure'. In reality we make our own luck. The first step is to want strongly something to happen. The second is to see opportunities when they arise, and grasp them.

To identify what it is that you really want to have or to

change in your life, spend a few minutes now making a list. Don't stop and ponder, just write spontaneously the first thoughts that come to mind.

I did this once. My husband had recently died and I really didn't know what I wanted to do with the rest of my life. Taking a sheet of paper I drew a vertical line down the centre. On the left-hand side I wrote all the things I wanted to do, irrespective of cost, location or commitment – much as I am suggesting you do now. Then on the right-hand side of my piece of paper I wrote down what I thought I *had* to do.

When I looked at this list the first thing that astonished me was that earning a living wasn't there. And I had always thought I enjoyed my job!

So why was I working? I asked myself. The answer was that I had to pay the mortgage, support and bring up my family and provide a living for those who were employed by me. Then I recognized that if I was prepared to lower my standard of living, get rid of the car, do without holidays, and so on, I need not work – or at any rate not to the same degree.

The question presented itself again. Why was I working? The job was stressful and put me under great pressure. I mulled these thoughts over for a while and then decided that having given my children a certain standard of living, I did not have the right to change that, but must wait until they were independent before doing anything too drastic.

Looking at my list of things I *wanted* to do with my life, I saw that with a little ingenuity, courage and determination, I could take some of the items on that list and actually make a living out of combining them.

My desire fired my enthusiasm. I sold the business to a caring company who guaranteed work for the staff. Then I retrained and entered the world of helping people with emotional and behavioural problems and . . . well, here I am!

Now having made your own list of the things you want to change or to happen in your life, I want you to write alongside each one all the advantages.

Your list may look something like this.

- Changing my job — Will be happier

- Making my children do more in the house — Won't feel taken for granted

- Treating myself sometimes — Will feel special

- Telling my partner of my needs when we make love — Will enjoy sex more

- Explaining to my boss when he fails to communicate — Will feel less stressed

The difference between these and previous thoughts of change you may have had, is that you are now looking at all the positives.

Usually, what prevents us from being assertive and voicing our needs, dislikes and fears, is that we anticipate negative results. *They won't understand. People won't like me. It will cause an uproar. I can't cope with confrontation. It isn't worth the fuss.*

You will never know unless you try. Pandering to other people's expectations of you diminishes you and prevents you from recognizing your true worth.

I recall a client who came to see me because she had reached breaking point in her relationship with her husband. Quite frankly, he treated her like a doormat. She recognized this but could see no way out.

'You see, he needs me,' she explained. 'I've done everything for him for so long he wouldn't be able to cope without me.'

In a way, her place in his life had become important to her – it made her feel needed. At the same time she hated herself for playing such a demeaning role.

After several consultations with her, she suddenly announced one day that she knew what she was going to do. Encouraged and supported by her adult children, she left the husband and moved in with one of her daughters.

I saw her some years later and she told me how good life was. She had managed to get a secretarial job and felt happy and fulfilled, and was financially independent. Her husband had remarried. 'The extraordinary thing is that he has chosen a really bossy woman who has him waiting on her hand and foot,' she told me, and then gave me a quick smile. 'Perhaps that's what he needed all the time.'

Allowing a dictator, bully, egotist or snob to continue with their illusion by supporting them, does no one any good. It may keep the peace – but at what cost?

It is unlikely that you are going to change your whole life overnight. However, by looking at your list, you will see one or two things that do need your immediate attention. If only for your health or peace of mind you need to do something about them *now*.

Once you have recognized this, actively begin to build your desire. Picture often how you will behave and how you will feel when you have made those changes. Be positive. Enhance the pictures with your imagination. Whenever you think of the objective of your desire, add to your list any positive thoughts that present themselves to you.

Remember, anything is possible and it all starts in your mind.

Belief

In order to follow through and turn your desire into reality the next required ingredient is belief. *You have to believe it is possible.*

Our doubts are often linked to a sense of poor self-esteem. *Why should it happen to me? I'm not worth it. I've never been any good at anything.* Who said so? Was it a parent? Teacher? Friend? Older brother or sister? Or have you been telling yourself this for so long that you actually believe it to be true?

It's sometimes easier to play safe and stay where you are than to risk rocking the boat. But is that what you truly want? Whatever conditioning you had during your childhood, you are now an adult with the ability and the right to make your own decisions about who you are and where you are going.

Sometimes you may feel that the way you are is due to someone else, and there is little you can do about it. Negative thoughts begin to bombard your mind: *My father ruined any chance I might ever have had to be good at maths. I had this boyfriend who destroyed my confidence. I can't, the family would never understand.*

Blame is a cop-out. Blame is a way of passing the responsibility on to someone else. Whenever we do this we become helpless, for we have told ourselves that we can't do anything about it, it is someone else's fault or responsibility. Blaming another takes away our ability or opportunity to do anything about a situation.

Whatever we believe determines the results we achieve. You have to believe in *something*, so why not the best that is available to you.

Exercise Two – Cutting the Cord

This exercise is to help you identify past incidents in your life that have had a lasting effect on the way you now feel and respond. A visual exercise then follows to help set you free.

Try doing this in the evening when you have half an hour to spend – it will surely be more productive than watching television. Remember, if it helps, you can always record the exercise onto a cassette, lie back in a comfortable chair, and simply listen.

A short relaxation exercise is given at the beginning of all future exercises, but where you feel the need for more time to relax, please feel free to use the induction given in Exercise One.

1 Breath deeply, close your eyes and relax. Spend a few moments mentally checking over your body, starting with your toes. As you become aware of each part of you, let it relax. To help you achieve this sense of complete relaxation, imagine yourself in a very peaceful, restful place – this could be in a room in your own home, on a beach, walking in a woodland, lying in the bath.

2 When you are feeling comfortable and relaxed, let your mind drift effortlessly back through your life until you reach an incident you feel may be responsible for holding you back and preventing you from making change – something that is responsible for restricting or influencing you in a negative way. See it on a screen in your mind. As you look at this, begin to understand why you reacted in the way you did.

3 Now see yourself physically tied to that picture by a cord. This cord is tying you to the past. Cut the cord and

set yourself free. Watch the picture fade away. Let it go completely.

4 Experience the sense of freedom.

Note: Whatever picture presents itself to you, deal with it. Some people tell me they feel as if they are in a glass jar, looking out at the world but unable to participate. If this is how you feel, smash the jar. If you feel as if there are cords tying you to the past, cut them. If you imagine a large stumbling block in your way, throw it over the edge of a cliff. *You don't have to live in the past or let it control you any longer.*

I had one client whose choice of visualization took her to a beach. Her problem was that she always felt threatened, as if she was being followed. Because of this she never dared go out alone. On the beach, in her imagination, she confronted two boys from her schooldays who used to do just that – follow her for the sheer hell of it. She dug a big hole in the sand and buried them. Drastic, but it worked. And it only needed to take place in her imagination!

Exercise Three – Clearing Out the Attic

Here is another way of dealing with a past that has been inhibiting you or holding you back.

1 Close your eyes, breathe deeply and relax. Now picture yourself going into an attic. There is a large skylight in the roof so that the attic is filled with sunlight. A lot of old junk clutters this room; some holds pleasant memories – old photos, a toy from your childhood,

something you made at school. But you recognize that there is also a lot of junk you no longer need or want.

2 Begin to sort out and clear away the rubbish. Whatever comes to mind, deal with it in a way that seems appropriate to you. Keep what you need at this moment in your life; the rest you can cart outside and burn. Have a really lovely bonfire. (While you are doing this at a conscious level, your unconscious mind, which is responsible for emotions and memories, will be dealing with other things from the past that need to be resolved.)

3 When you have finished, picture yourself a little into the future, and feeling so much better about yourself – you are much more positive and happy. Add colour, sound, smells, taste, the texture of things – anything that helps the experience to become real. Pay attention to how you feel.

4 Open your eyes, take a deep breath, hold on to those positive feelings.

Note: You may need to repeat this visual exercise several times until the attic feels just the way you want it to be.

I remember doing this exercise myself and finding only empty cartons. I cleared them out and had a glorious bonfire. It was only afterwards that I realized the significance of what I had pictured. As I had found only empty boxes, there was nothing to hold me back! Being made out of cardboard, I had no problem in totally demolishing what had contained my past negative experiences.

Now the path is clear, you are ready to move forward and get on with your life. By using your imagination and focusing on all the positives, you can work at building your desire; you can actively begin to believe that you can make things happen. You are no longer the victim.

Of course some of the things you do may upset the apple cart a bit for other people. However, if you go about this in the right way, not only will you feel a whole lot better, but you will also be opening doors for them. If they are ready, they will recognize the opportunity – and may even get around to thanking you one day for setting things in motion.

Let's look at what can happen.

I have a friend who always gets upset when her husband's family visits. She is one of those people who makes a real effort. Washing her hair, making-up carefully and putting on a nice dress is her way of welcoming them. The husband always laughs at this and ridicules her in front of his family. To add to this they join him in making her feel silly and small. She doesn't want to change. This is the way she is and she sees it as demonstrating to them that they are special and she is prepared to make an effort to entertain them.

Together we looked at what would happen if she told them how hurt she was by their behaviour. She had attempted on several occasions to tell her husband but he didn't want to know and made no effort to understand her feelings.

'It couldn't be any worse,' she decided. 'So I'll do what you suggest. I'll try first to get my husband to sit down and really listen.'

Before doing this she visually cut herself free from pictures of past visits from his family when she had felt ridiculed; she also wiped out pictures of her husband's previous refusals to understand or listen. Mentally she rehearsed the conversation they would have, how she was going to explain her feelings, and all the good results that would come from doing this.

It worked so well that when next the family came, the

husband washed, shaved and dressed in a clean shirt and trousers. No one joked. His support left no room for ridicule. And, interestingly, on the following visit, everyone made a real effort to dress up. It felt like a party. They all enjoyed themselves and, thereafter, what had seemed ridiculous became the norm.

A very different kind of story demonstrating the same point is of a man who was training to be an accountant. He was having serious trouble in passing his finals, but felt under terrible pressure to stay in his job as he had a wife and two small children to support.

After looking at all his options, he decided to dare to talk to his wife about the way he felt. He was very much afraid that this would cause him to be diminished in her sight. He didn't know how he would cope with failure, but he did know he couldn't go on the way he was feeling. The exams, he realized, were not the real issue – he was in the wrong kind of job.

To his surprise, his wife expressed only concern for him. She had seen for a long time what was wrong but hadn't known how to tell him.

For three years they reversed roles. She went back to her old job and supported the family financially, while he stayed home, cared for the children and retrained as a draughtsman.

It is sad to think he was stressed for so long because he believed that there was no way out.

Sometimes making change can benefit everyone. Life is not about keeping up appearances or how things look to others. How we feel inside is what really matters. When we refuse to submit to fear, we set ourselves free. Our destiny lies within our own hands, it does not belong to anyone else.

Tim is a friend of mine. Before I knew him, he suffered from severe depression and had attempted to take his life on a number of occasions. Doctors had finally given up on him. He had had electroconvulsive therapy and spent many months in a psychiatric hospital. Finally he was discharged and told that there was nothing else they could do for him.

He was on his own. He climbed into his car and drove away from the only place where he had felt safe. There was only one thing left for him to do. This time he would drive off the edge of a high bridge into the river. There would be no going back, he was determined to end his miserable life.

Tim sat all night in his car. He watched the dawn break. He heard the birds begin to sing. *He could not drive off that bridge*. It was then he realized that until he stopped using the thought of suicide as an escape, he was never going to get better. If life was ever to be worth living it was up to him to make it so. No one else could do it for him.

Tim succeeded. He is one of the kindest, most compassionate men I know. He realizes that he has learned from all his suffering: none of it was in vain. He sees purpose in everything now and believes that everything can work for good – if he will allow it to.

There is good in every experience. Your belief needs to be like Tim's. Nothing is ever wasted. Every experience is a learning one – we need only to be awakened to it.

To every negative there is a positive. This is the law of the universe.

Rain may prevent you from gardening, but you can catch up on indoor jobs or just enjoy curling up in front of the fire with a good book.

Losing your job can open the door to other opportunities – perhaps going back to college to learn something you have always wanted to do. This would then be turning a negative experience into a positive one.

The loss of a loved one can lead to a greater understanding of suffering, and may motivate us to raise funds to help in a special area of medicine or science. Losing a loved one can set us free to do something we might never have envisaged before.

Looking purposefully for the positives in everything will help you to build your belief system. Remember, there is good in all things.

Expectation

Before any action can take place, thought must initiate it. Think about something, enhance it with your imagination, and then allow the feelings related to that thought to take root – to be experienced. Allowing yourself to feel how it will be is a powerful motivator.

You are then ready to act. The surprising thing is that in many cases it is sufficient to simply allow the thought and feelings to surface – the result will quite often manifest itself without any further effort on your part.

Quite recently I was talking with great enthusiasm to a group of friends about white chrysanthemums. I had actually had a very vivid dream about this perfect flower with its flawless, white curved petals; I had felt the firm edges of the green stalk between my fingers and smelt the unique perfume. I wanted to share my experience.

The very next morning one of those friends arrived carrying a pot of white chrysanthemums. 'I just wanted you to enjoy the real thing,' she said. Well, I already had. Nothing could have been more real than that dream. But I was delighted – not only because I now owned the plant, but also because this had enabled me to see clearly the power of thought at work.

When I was managing an engineering plant I had many similar experiences. Often my partner and I would look at the order book and see that we were rapidly catching up with the existing orders. When you have machinery manufacturing millions of components an hour, it is a very serious situation to actually overtake the order book. You then have to decide whether to let the machine run on, change to another size, or stop the machine.

My partner and I would look at each other and nod. Then one of us would say, 'There'll be an order in the post tomorrow.' There always was.

To be successful it is essential to cultivate positive expectation. From wishing for something we move to *desiring*, and from desiring to *believing* it to be a real possibility. We then open the third door by using *expectation*.

Expectation is a very powerful force. It really does seem to make things happen. I have found, however, that things never seem to happen when we allow anxious feelings or fear to cloud the horizon – the negative thoughts cancel out the positive.

Expectation must be unconditional. It needs to be a confident, glorious, joyful *knowing* that it will be so.

When you expect something to happen and it doesn't appear in the form you had anticipated, try to see how your expectation is being met in another direction.

Going back to my own experiences in the factory, we were once so focused on anticipating a large order for small bar-turned components (which, incidentally, did not materialize) that we almost missed the opportunity to open a welding shop and make caravan fittings. This proved to be a far better product with a much longer life – and we nearly missed it because we failed to see what was being offered to us.

If your expectation is worthy of you it will never fail. Your positive attitude will actually have an influence. How this works no one quite knows, but we do know that 'thought waves', acting like small electronic impulses, do not stop at the skull but go on out into the world, where they may be picked up by someone in the right receptive mode.

It is almost as if someone is sitting at his desk saying, 'I wonder who could do this job for us?' and whizz, along comes your thought.

How often have you thought about someone and minutes later you receive a phone call from them, or a letter arrives by the next post? It happens far too often for even the most sceptical to brush it aside as coincidence.

The trouble is that we have been so conditioned by left-brain logic that we totally overlook the remarkable things that happen for which, as yet, we have no scientific explanation. There is, however, plenty of evidence to substantiate the belief that when we use the right-brain – the visual, intuitive side of the brain – we operate on a completely different level. (More about this in Chapter 14 when we look at being creative.)

Our expectation can often give us the edge we need to clinch a deal or to achieve something that is of value to us.

A friend of mine who works as a retail manager tells me that once a sales representative gets inside his office, if he likes him, his mind shifts from why *not* to buy his product to why he *should* buy it. What has happened here is that the salesman's expectant attitude defies disappointment. He may not get an order at every outlet, but by the end of the week he will have scored far higher than the man who expects to be turned away.

To get what we want is dependent on what we believe we deserve. You have to be willing to let your life be a success; it isn't by accident or luck that people excel or achieve their goals, it is *by design*. They plan it that way, and focus on their goals and achievements, *not* on failure or disappointment. In this way failures really do turn into challenges and everything becomes an experience from which we can learn.

No one, but no one, is going to get everything they want in life without having learning experiences – it's the way our world works.

Sadly, many people are so busy keeping score of all the misfortunes, hardships and bad experiences they believe they have had, that they fail to capitalize on them by using them productively.

The same thing can often be seen at work in people who always believe there is something wrong with them – they will even label themselves as unlucky, and in believing this they allow bad things to happen. This endorses their belief. Not only do they become very tedious and boring to others, but they miss all the things that are good in their lives.

I have a friend who recently had a heart operation. Afterwards, for a considerable time, he felt unwell and quite depressed. Then one day he met an old friend who had had a similar operation. 'You need to hold your head up high and walk tall; step out as if nothing is wrong with you,' his friend advised. After only *one* day, my friend reported that he did feel very much better.

Staying ill is sometimes a way of getting attention; it can make people feel important. But it is such a waste of lives that could be gloriously fulfilled and purposeful. The trouble is that such people often reach a point where they are convinced that there really *is* something wrong with them, or they are afraid of doing anything in case the old illness returns.

In my book *Are You in Control?*, I talk of being 'attractive' and name it 'happiness'. Happiness is the most attractive of all human qualities and is freely available to all of us. It draws people to us. Happy people are more successful at getting what they want. Doing something for someone who responds with joy and happiness is far more rewarding than doing it for someone who responds with moans and groans and is never satisfied.

Happy people *expect* nice things to happen – and they usually do.

Positive Expectation

There was once an old woman who lived in the outback of Canada. Winter was coming but she was now too old to cut or gather her own fuel. Each day, a neighbour passing by would comment on her empty store.

'What are you going to do about it?' he asked.

She smiled gently. 'God will provide,' she answered.

The days passed into weeks, the temperature dropped, soon the snow would fall and it would be too late to do anything about the fuel she needed.

Still she smiled confidently and assured her neighbour that God would provide.

One morning she heard a noise outside the house. On opening the door she saw the neighbour unloading logs into her store.

'Well, God wasn't doing anything about it,' he told her. 'So I thought I'd better.'

She smiled her thanks and nodded. She had known all along that God, in his own way, would provide.

Negative Expectation

There was a man (I'll call him Jack) who was a keen gardener. The season was progressing but his work in the garden had been held up by poor weather conditions. He knew that he really had to get the plants from the green-house into the garden that weekend.

The weather forecast, however, was bad. If rain came and made the soil too heavy he would be unable to work it. Jack kept wandering outside and looking up at the clouds, waiting for it to rain. He felt morose and that his weekend had been a failure.

On Monday morning, back at work, his colleague asked: 'Did you get your garden done?' 'How could I?'

he responded. 'Didn't you hear the weather forecast?'

'But it was a good day for gardening on Sunday,' his colleague said. 'I got all my plants out.'

Jack was so filled with negative expectation that he totally missed the opportunity.

Never underestimate the power of expectation.

2

The Child Within

In all of us there remains the child. In many ways this is good. The child within allows us to discard the sober cloak of adulthood and responsibility sometimes and to become as a child again.

Children have fun. Children can feel and act with complete abandon. Children don't spoil today by fretting about tomorrow. They have learned how to live in the 'now'. We need children around us as a constant reminder of how life should be lived. The trouble with all of us is that we prevent ourselves from enjoying what we have by worrying about what we don't have or what might go wrong.

One of my friends once said to me, 'I gave up worrying about tomorrow long ago. I realized that most of the things we get upset about never happen anyway.'

I have learned more from my children and grandchildren than from all the books I've read, or courses I've attended. Children teach us how to be young at heart again; they know what really matters. But there is also the child within us that needs to be set free; the sad, fearful, angry, or guilty child who hides behind the adult facade.

How often have you found, in certain situations, that you revert to a childish response?

Flying into a temper over small unimportant things . . .

Let's look at some examples.

- Arguing that you're right
- Flying into a temper over small unimportant things
- Boasting about achievements
- Getting upset when you can't have your own way
- Demanding attention
- Feeling hurt when you are overlooked or ignored
- Sulking
- Refusing to speak or to listen
- Wanting to get back at someone

There are probably plenty more you can recognize in yourself, or in others, that you could add to this list.

Certain people and various situations do seem to have the unhappy knack of bringing out those childish responses in us. What happens is that we suffer a re-stimulation or reminder of a past experience that we have never learned how to handle in a mature manner.

An authoritative figure reminding you of a teacher you once feared, can have you cringing or acting in a submissive manner when that isn't what you want to be doing at all. In fact, if the feelings are very powerful, this 'leftover' response can have you allowing just about everyone to walk all over you.

A parent from whom you failed to gain approval during your childhood, can still have you running around at the age of 50 or 60 struggling for the praise that was never there.

This part of the child within needs desperately to be released, for it is impossible to go forward while clinging to the past.

However, emotions are not rational. You may *know* very well what you *ought* to be doing about it, but you don't know *how*.

The first step is to recognize where and how your present behaviour is being controlled by past experiences. There is usually a trigger point – one painful incident that you can recall. This may have been strengthened by further experiences, all adding to your sense of failure and a desperate need to please.

A dictatorial father may have been gentle and doting while you were a baby, but you can only remember the high, demanding standards he set upon you as a child. Failing to live up to those impossible expectations may well have caused you to label yourself as useless or stupid.

I knew of a man who, when his children reached the age of ten, formally announced that there was to be no more kissing. They were now too old for that sort of thing, he informed them. His daughter later told me: 'There must have been a time when he did kiss us, but I can't remember it.' This was her trigger point. It was at this moment she experienced the rejection that was to spoil all later relationships. She was never going to let anyone get close enough to hurt her again.

Taking Care of the Child Within

I would like you to imagine for the next few minutes that someone once entrusted you with the upbringing of a baby. To start with you had help and could draw on other people's experiences. Gradually, as the child grew, you became more and more involved in shaping that young life and received less help and advice from others.

You began to teach the child values; trust and courage were built; there were times when the child underwent painful experiences from which it learned a lot about life.

As you allow your imagination to encompass the idea of caring for this young life, tell yourself how you would guide the child. How would you show your love and caring?

You would have given encouragement, support, praise. Quite rightly, you would have felt pride. Perhaps sometimes you may have wanted to give more than was good for the child – you had to learn wisdom and moderation. Nothing would have been too much trouble.

By now you are probably thinking, *I know all this!* Probably you have already brought up a child, cared for someone, or been involved with children in some way. What I want you to realize is that you have had this experience in a very *different* way. The hypothetical child whose life and well-being was entrusted to you, was yourself. And did you honestly give to yourself as much love, caring, patience, understanding, encouragement and praise as you would to another?

The answer is probably *No*. For the truth is that for most of us, our own fulfilment in life is not given priority; it is often treated as secondary to almost everyone else's needs. Most of the time we fail to give any consideration to our own needs, we are so busy trying to please everyone else. But surely you deserve as much consideration, love and caring as our hypothetical baby? Why should you be singled out as being unworthy? How many times have you given praise and credit to another while pouring scorn on your own similar efforts?

Without even stopping to think about it, we tend to grind ourselves into the dust while using endless energy supporting and encouraging others.

You would probably never tell another person, *You look a mess*, or *You're useless*, or *You'll never be any good at . . .* I wouldn't mind betting, though, that you have told yourself these, or similar words, dozens of times.

How much do you value yourself, your time, your feelings, your beliefs? Do you realize that when you treat yourself badly you encourage others to do the same?

How much do you love yourself? Loving yourself says that you are lovable; it invites people to treat you with tenderness and caring. See yourself as a perfect creation. Isn't it marvellous the way you can use your sight, your voice, your sense of smell? Isn't it fantastic the way your body works? Each bone, muscle, nerve, organ, cell of your body is a miracle of life. You are a wonderful human being. Think of the complex thoughts and feelings you are capable of experiencing. You are touched by beauty. You feel awe, joy, tenderness, love. How can you be all these things and not love yourself?

It's time to go back and give that child within the words and love you failed to give it in the past.

Exercise Four – Comforting the Child Within

1 Close your eyes and relax. Let your mind drift back to your childhood. Perhaps you can recall a place where you used to play at a certain age – this may be your bedroom, on a swing, in a garden, at your grandparents' house. Build in your mind a picture of your surroundings –

include sounds, smells, and the feel of things. Take your time.

2 Notice how old you are in this picture. What you are wearing? Are you alone, or is there a brother, sister or playmate with you? How are you feeling?

3 Now allow yourself to recall a time when you felt upset as a child. Perhaps you were teased, rejected, laughed at, wrongly accused or punished for something you did not do.

4 As you picture this child that you were, imagine now that as a mature, caring adult, you talk to the child, comforting and reassuring your younger self. Say the words he or she needs to hear.

5 Place your arms around the child. Hold him/her close. As you hold the child you may even feel it merge with you as you become one.

6 Stay with this picture until the bad feelings fade. Experience a feeling of peace. Let go of the past that has been hurting.

7 Slowly open your eyes, breathe deeply, and think now about yourself as a complete human being capable of loving and being loved.

Note: You may find that this visualization can make you feel very upset. If this is so, let the emotions out; they have been bottled up for far too long. If you feel it will help, discuss your experience with a trusted friend. Where you feel you cannot cope with them, it is important that you seek professional counselling or guidance.

Parents often instil in us a sense of failure when what they really mean to do is spur us on to greater things. To have an older brother or sister held up as a shining example, usually only serves to make us feel inferior or inadequate.

We don't *have* to be like anyone else to be successful; we only have to be the best we are personally capable of being as ourselves. There is no way you can run, smile, do maths or write like any other person – you do it your way.

One of the reasons our educational system fails so many youngsters is that they are all taught in the same manner. But we don't all learn in the same way. Depending on which of the senses is dominant, some children learn by 'seeing', some by 'doing', some by 'hearing'; some will need to use all three senses to make up a whole experience.

Do not base your success on being like other people – no matter what you were told as a child.

The truth is that when we don't know how to respond, we revert to the childhood behaviour that seemed to get the best results.

To develop a more satisfying and mature way of dealing with your responses, try using an 'anchor'. This means choosing the response you would rather have, and then using a signal to re-stimulate those better feelings in that situation.

For example, you may choose to be quietly determined instead of yelling, losing your temper, bursting into tears, or breaking something.

Here's how it works.

Exercise Five – Changing Responses

The example we are going to take is one where you wish you could exercise calm determination but find yourself getting frustrated and yelling.

1 Recall a moment when you have experienced quiet

determination – it can relate to any time at all. It may be that you recall learning to ride a bicycle, drive a car, make something in woodwork, sew a dress. No matter how much effort was required or how long it took, you were quietly determined to complete the task. As you think about this, allow those feelings to return. Now gently press the palm of one hand to your forehead. Hold it there for a few seconds and then place your hand back in your lap and relax.

2 Now picture a time recently when you found yourself using an old childish response – yelling, perhaps, or getting frustrated.

3 As those childlike feelings return, press your palm once more to your forehead and allow the better feelings to take over.

4 Tell yourself that from now on you will use this signal (anchor) to put yourself in control, to enable you to use quiet determination.

5 Slowly open your eyes, breathe deeply, and remember to put into action this new behaviour. The more you apply it, the easier it will become to use your chosen responses.

You can, of course, choose any feeling to substitute for another, and any kind of signal will do. Instead of pressing your palm to your forehead you could clasp your hands together, or press a finger nail into your palm, or take three deep breaths, or even sing a tune. Smells are very good anchors to certain feelings although not really appropriate to this exercise – but in everyday life they happen naturally.

When reading this book, always feel free to take the principle behind the exercise and apply it to your own individual experiences.

3

Wishing You Were Someone Else

If you have ever looked upon another person and wished you were him or her, this needs to be dealt with before you can commence your *daring* journey. Do you honestly want to be someone else? Or do you want to do better at being yourself and achieve similar goals?

Wishing to be someone else is usually a longing to escape from the invisible shackles that prevent you from daring to be yourself. It is also an unconscious admission that you see no possibility of ever achieving certain goals in life by being yourself. Where you find you are actually wishing you were someone else, ask yourself what it is about the other person that you find so attractive.

Are they financially successful? And is it the material gains or the success you desire?

Do you wish to be loved, respected and admired as is this other person?

Do you long to be someone you know who has children? If you are unable, for whatever reason, to have a family of your own, there is so much you can do for children who need people like you. Follow this path and you could well find yourself with more loving arms around you than you ever bargained for.

Look for the reason behind your desire. You can achieve and become successful in your own right. Once you have set yourself free from limiting beliefs, the world is yours. It is waiting for you and you have as much right to a share in all the good things as any other person.

Sometimes wishing you were someone else is an unconscious desire to escape from what you see as a way of life that has become intolerable. Here you need to identify specifically what it is in your own life that you can no longer bear.

Kelly was an example of someone who always wanted to be someone else – in this case, me. I appeared to have all the things she had ever longed for – a loving family, a caring mother, job satisfaction. In contrast, she was an only child and her mother, sadly, was an alcoholic.

Eventually Kelly made a decision to do something about her life. She recognized that her mother was never going to change – her life was ruled by alcohol – so Kelly left home and went to work in an old people's nursing home. She lavished her love on these old people, giving each of them a morning hug and a goodnight kiss when she tucked them up for the night.

Everyone loved her. She told me that she had never been so happy in her life. When Kelly stopped wanting to be me and did something about her own life she got far more out of it than she had ever dreamed possible.

Below is a list of words that we regularly use to describe others yet find more difficult to apply to ourselves (written at random exactly as they came to mind).

Confident	Artistic
Attractive	Assertive
Poised	Clever
Slim	Successful

Knowledgeable	Logical
Charming	Calm
Eloquent	Relaxed
Creative	

The good news is that you can be all of these – some natural attributes need only to be recognized and then allowed to blossom; others will require hard work and dedication. For most of us, wanting a university degree means years of study and research, but it is possible. Often a vague, wistful feeling lurks beneath the surface, only we are not sufficiently motivated to do anything about it.

Almost everyone would like to be successful in some area of life. Having plenty of money is a dream shared by millions – the tantalizing offers to get rich quick would never continue to drop through the letterbox if people didn't have this yearning.

We think there is some magic ingredient to acquiring a fortune, or being successful, and we all look for some justification for being a failure or victim. There is no such thing as failure, it is only a point of view. To take a good hard look at the reality of failure, the nearest you can get to it is by never having tried.

What we do have in abundance, and which are the privilege and right of every human being, are learnt experiences. They are so precious and invaluable, but most of the time we brush them aside as failures or bad luck.

Do not allow the success of others to dishearten you. Be inspired by their example and use this as a spur towards being your true self, achieving your own goals, and enjoying your own successes.

Much of our negative thinking and attitudes come from past experiences and indoctrination: girls born into certain cultures are still being taught that they are inferior. Suppose those girls were transported into a tribe of Amazonian women – what then? They are still the same sex, so what has changed? *The way they are taught to value themselves*.

Even in the Western world many women are still struggling against the belief that their role is in the home and that they have inferior brain power.

We all know that teasing and ridicule can have a devastating effect upon us emotionally. Such experiences can influence how we see and value ourselves, and is very destructive. When we are young and vulnerable and made to feel inferior, we are likely to carry that feeling with us for the rest of our life.

There are few of us who have not, from time to time, wished we could achieve things we see or hear of others doing.

When I speak with clients who are depressed, I ask them if there isn't something they have longed to have a go at. They reply with comments such as, *I always wanted to play the piano* or *I would have liked to paint – or travel – or learn to swim*. Then they go on to tell me that they never tried because they knew they would be no good at it.

They see other people succeeding but prevent themselves from ever trying with negative beliefs. How do you know until you have tried? You don't have to excel in order to enjoy playing the piano or painting.

Wishing you were someone else takes away the responsibility. It also relieves you from making the effort. You need to get this very firmly lodged in your head: you don't have to be someone else, you only have to be yourself doing that thing – if that's what you wish.

Many fears come from what we see as failure at school. The truth usually is that if the pupil hasn't learnt, the fault lies in the teaching method. Often teachers simply do not have time to help each child individually. Sometimes they are just bad teachers. You may recall how well you did in a class where you liked the teacher. When we are happy and relaxed we learn best. Take heart, all that is behind you. As a mature adult you can now do anything you choose – if you truly want to.

This book is about learning to recognize your value, your uniqueness, and then applying that learning to every minute of the rest of your life.

4

Letting Go of Illusions

An illusion is a deceptive impression of reality. We can be so deceived that we have no knowledge or awareness that what we perceive is not exactly as we believe it to be. That is why letting go of your illusions can be so frightening; for a while it may seem as if you are lost, floundering in unknown territory. The artificial belief system you have been using to support you is swept away. It may feel as if everything you have lived for suddenly becomes worthless, and these thoughts can be very painful.

However, the results, and the 'new you' that emerges, make all the pain of change worthwhile.

Erica's Story

When Erica was still a very small child, her parents' marriage broke up. The mother went to live in Australia and Erica was taken care of by her grandparents.

As she grew older, she came to believe in her own mind that her parents had left her because they did not love her. Because she believed this, she also believed that she was unlovable – no mother would leave her baby without a very good reason.

To endorse her beliefs, Erica couldn't love herself either. By the age of 14 she weighed 12 stone. The more she ate the worse she felt. *No wonder no one liked her!* she thought. It was quite impossible to get through to Erica that she had some wonderful qualities that made her likeable and that one could admire.

Visiting her was difficult, to say the least. Whatever one said, if she could possibly find a way of turning it around so that she saw it as a slight, ridicule or criticism, she did so. One dared not mention anyone else's appearance in front of her – she always saw it as a way of getting at her. Food, sport and exercise could not be mentioned.

Constructive advice such as invitations to join a swimming group, exercise or yoga class were all converted by her mind into negative feelings about herself. She could not see that it was because we loved her and cared about her that we wanted to help.

It became easier to avoid her. When Erica realized people were avoiding her, she was convinced it was because she was fat and people didn't like her. Their very behaviour was proof to her that she had been right all along.

Then Erica's mother returned, and set about establishing a relationship with her daughter. Now Erica desperately needed that. She tried to accept the story her mother told her of how impossible it had been for her to continue living with her father. But the emotional part of her could not trust; she was afraid to get close in case her mother disappeared again.

Finally Erica found her way to my consulting rooms. By then she was married and had two normal, healthy children. She had a lovely face and complexion and above average intelligence. She ought to have found happiness at last, but by now she believed all her problems were because she was so overweight. The truth had very successfully been hidden beneath layers of fat.

No one could have helped Erica until she was ready to let go of the illusion and face the reality.

Norman's Story

Norman's story is very different, and demonstrates the problem of illusion from another angle. He believed that if he was very clever and knowledgeable, read all the 'right' books and mixed with the 'right' people he would find respect and a favourable position in life.

All credit to him, he worked and studied for hours while the other boys were out having a good time. He went to university (something his parents had never dreamed could happen to one of their sons) and attained a degree. From there Norman went into banking. At the age of 34 he became manager of a large bank in the Midlands. Socializing was important and entertaining was done on a lavish scale – always with what Norman saw as the *right* people. It wasn't until Norman was close to retirement that he discovered, much to his surprise, that he had no real friends. No one seemed to want his company unless there was something in it for them.

Unconsciously, the message he had sent out to those people whose friendship and company he craved was that he was better than they were – better read, better dressed, better informed, better spoken. He might have ended his days still living his illusion and wondering what had gone wrong with his world, but for his brother George – an ordinary guy who worked as a garage mechanic.

Norman's brother loved him enough to risk shattering his illusions. He took Norman on holiday where they mixed with people from all walks of life. Norman noticed how popular his brother was with everyone, how the atmosphere changed in a pub when George walked in.

Curious, he finally asked his brother what was the secret of his popularity.

'I just like people,' George told him.

Norman was silent for some time after this. As he faced the truth he let his illusions about what was important and what mattered fall from him. It wasn't doing everything he could do to impress others and make them like him that worked, *it was liking other people!*

It is hard *not* to build illusions. Television does an excellent job of helping us create illusions about ourselves and others: buy a certain diet drink and you will become slim and attractive and be loved by tall dark handsome men; impress your friends by using a particular brand of floor cleaner or air freshener, or buying certain furniture. It seems that to be happy and enjoy life, you need to buy whatever it is they want to sell.

Of course we aren't complete fools: chocolate doesn't taste better if you have beautiful pouting lips, and certain brands of wine aren't only available to the poised upper class. Advertising, though, is so subtle that we unconsciously read the message telling us where we fall short of the standards that are acceptable to the rest of our world – and this illusion helps to sell the products!

How many overweight women continue to feel attractive after advertising has bombarded their senses? How many men believe they are attractive when they lose their hair or develop a paunch? Advertising's visual images, subtly presented, tell you that you need to do something about yourself.

I'm not knocking all advertising – we can all feel good about wearing glasses or dentures since the small screen started promoting them; even menstruation, which used to be considered unmentionable, is now presented in attractive advertisements with neat packages of sanitary protection. But for the most part, advertising makes us very dissatisfied with the way we are.

To avoid facing what we are, we hide behind hobbies, work, alcohol, drugs, relationships – *anything* that stops us thinking about life and who we are. *I'm too busy; I haven't got time; I don't feel too good; I'm on holiday* – there's a thousand ways of hiding. But now and again other thoughts surface: *What is life all about? What am I doing here?*

Having something physically wrong with you is a very acceptable way of hiding behind an illusion. People are kind to you, they don't make demands, you don't have to do anything you don't want to.

I recall being on a course where we were looking at ways to use hypnosis to identify the cause of pain and how to deal with it. A doctor announced that he had a very painful area in his foot that prevented him from doing things. He had tried cortisone injections and various other treatments without success. He was asked to allow himself to go to alpha level (a mentally relaxed state where positive suggestion takes effect) and to ask his unconscious mind why he had this problem. The answer came at once: *It's my excuse.* When he didn't want

What is life all about?

to do something and didn't like to refuse, the foot always conveniently offered him a way out – it prevented him from doing that thing. What was surprising, even to him, was that he had not recognized this and had genuinely experienced pain.

The happy end to this story is that he chose an alternative way of dealing with the problem. '*I'll just say no,*' he said. A month later he was able to report that the pain had completely disappeared.

Believing that people will like us better if we try to be someone that we are not, is an illusion shared by many. Why are we so afraid of being ourselves? What has brought about this fear of revealing our true selves? Does it result from constant criticism as a child, or from teasing and bullying? Or is it perhaps failure to appreciate one's own unique contribution to life?

Over the years we have become very good at covering up our true nature with illusions until we hardly know who we are. Most of the time this was done in order to avoid feeling pain, but the price we paid was high – we lost out on love. We forgot that we were of value, we stopped loving ourselves, we stopped trusting others. They say that if you tell yourself something often enough you end up believing it, and we have somehow tricked ourselves into believing that the pretences, the illusions and the lies are more important than the reality.

Remind yourself often that it is not important how you look but how you feel. When you allow others to become more important in your mind than yourself, then you begin to feel inferior. You lose the power to do anything about the way you are feeling.

We can't begin to change until we face the truth and see where we can become better at being ourselves rather than mimicking someone else, or trying to live up to what we believe is acceptable behaviour. Pretensions are not necessary when you like who you are, and the first requirement to self-improvement and daring to be yourself is to begin to love yourself.

Have you ever thought about a perfectionist? He fools himself into believing that he seeks perfection, when what he really does is to spend his life searching for flaws. Searching for the imperfections in order to ensure perfection prevents him from perceiving that which is good and beautiful and a joy to behold.

A colleague of mine was explaining why he dreaded Christmas. 'I spend a lot of time pretending to like the presents people have given to me, when most of the time I'll never use them or they are not what I would have chosen,' he said.

His wife looked up in surprise. 'But all presents are lovely,' she said, 'when you think how someone has gone out to carefully select something for you – well, I think it makes any present just wonderful.'

While he had been outwardly pretending that all was well with the gifts, and inwardly rejecting them, his wife had found the perfect answer. At that moment she made it possible for him to change his viewpoint.

You may be thinking that it is rude to behave in a way that forces people to face up to the pretence in their own lives, but if they are ready, your gentle persistence in refusing to support their illusions can help to revolutionize their life.

Try to avoid self-pity and don't encourage others to wallow in such destructive negative feelings by offering sympathy. Sympathy says, *It's okay to feel that way, I understand*. Empathy, on the other hand, is constructive. It means giving support while encouraging that person to release negative thoughts and feelings and to rise above them.

Hypochondriacs are a good example of this self-destruct mechanism. By being constantly sympathetic, asking how they are, saying how awful it must be for them, we only enable them to stay in that situation and do not help them to climb out of it. Far better to encourage them to try to take an interest in things outside their 'illness' and to attempt to live a normal, active life.

When my family was much younger our doctor called on me as I had developed mumps along with the children. I recall his words: 'You can feel sorry for yourself for a few days,' he said, 'then try getting up and doing things again.' He went on to tell me that he was on his way to visit a private patient who took to her bed when her husband died and had played the role of chronic invalid ever since. 'There is actually nothing wrong with her,' he told me. 'I wouldn't keep on going but she pays me.'

He was supporting her illusion. He was not helping her in any way to start living again. When I tell you that this situation had been going on for 13 years you will understand just how it appalled me.

If you find yourself wanting sympathy, ask yourself what it will achieve. Such feelings trap you and give you no hope of ever climbing out of that state.

Assuring the boss that his after-dinner speech was fine and everyone enjoyed it may boost his ego, but if this is untrue it definitely will not help him to improve. Much kinder to be honest and then leave it to him to decide how he could better his public speaking.

Most of the changes I have made in my life have been as a result of someone telling me honestly where I needed to take another look at the way I was doing something.

Time now to do an exercise on recognizing one or two of your own illusions and letting go of them.

Exercise Six – Dealing with Illusions

1 Make yourself comfortable, close your eyes and relax. Take a few very deep breaths and then mentally check

over your body, allowing each part of you to let go and relax. Now think about some behaviour or way you present yourself that does not feel comfortable to you. This could be your appearance: you may believe that expensive clothes are necessary if you are to get on in the world, but that is an illusion. You may feel that you have to behave in a subservient manner to people whom you see as important or influential – that is another illusion. You may feel you are inferior to people you see as being clever or better educated – another illusion. You may believe you have to speak without a certain accent in order to be taken seriously – one more illusion. You may feel that you have to agree with people in order to be liked or accepted – still another illusion.

2 Ask yourself why you get uncomfortable feelings when you behave in a certain way. Is it because you are acting a part and not being true to yourself? (This may be because you lack confidence.) Do you feel life will treat you more kindly if you act that way? Have you stopped trusting who you really are? Are you afraid that if you reveal your true self people will reject you? Are you afraid of being labelled stupid or unkind?

3 Having identified your feelings, can you see that they are controlled by illusions? No one is better than you, no one has more rights than you, and you do not need to try to be anything but what you are.

4 Imagine how it would feel if you let go of that illusion, or stopped supporting someone else's illusion, and behaved with complete honesty?

5 Do you feel better about yourself when you do this? Do you feel more at ease, less bored or intolerant? Move the images around in your mind until you feel happy with them.

Remember, this exercise is not about keeping everyone else happy but feeling better about the way you behave.

6 When you are ready to make this change, say quietly to yourself, *I can be completely honest with myself and with others. I only have to be myself.*

7 Slowly open your eyes, breathe deeply and feel good about your new resolution to be honest in your behaviour and in your treatment of others.

Note: Repeat this exercise daily for at least two weeks, seeing yourself using this new behaviour and stating your affirmations. It is best done at night when you are relaxed in bed just before you settle down to sleep.

An illusion can have been so successfully used that it is hard to see behind it. People are often so scared of revealing themselves that they go to ridiculous lengths to hide their uniqueness. They believe that they will only be accepted if they are like others. But it is hard work, and beneath the facade they feel disgusted with themselves.

Never bargain with your integrity. We hear of famous people who have done this – politicians, actors, millionaires. When exposed, they bluster, deny or run away. Can any man be his true self when he has violated his integrity? He may have acquired riches, but living in peace with himself is another matter altogether.

I was in the garden one day sitting talking to a very ambitious young lady who was convinced that you could talk anybody into doing anything. Being honest in business didn't work, she told me, it got you nowhere. You had to tell people what they wanted to hear.

A friend called unexpectedly and sat down to join us.

He listened to her in silence for some time and then said, 'Sarah, I have never met you before and the chances are that I never will again. So what I say to you is totally for your own good.'

She looked at him suspiciously. 'What is it?'

'Whatever face you show to others, whatever words you use, be true to yourself. Know who you really are and why you are doing whatever it is you are doing.'

She didn't understand what he was talking about. She had built a picture of the business world that was so untrue that she was totally out of touch with reality – and she couldn't see it.

That all happened ten years ago. John has gone from strength to strength and become very successful. Sarah's business failed and she is still blaming it on the previous recession and the bank's refusal to extend her overdraft.

You can be honest, truthful and just, and still succeed. Certainly you do not need to support other people in their illusions; by refusing to do so you are offering them a new awareness of who they really are and the opportunity to use their own uniqueness.

Pandering to other people is neither honest nor productive. It weakens them, and ultimately their self-deception will destroy them as people of value. Speaking and living in truth is the only way to live a life that is worthy of you.

When you hear someone complaining that everyone is always so thoughtless towards them, this should not be met with 'You poor thing. How awful!'

'Why do you think that is?' will hopefully initiate a response that leads to a meaningful conversation. Is the person's negativity perhaps responsible for driving people away?

I once knew someone who had no close friends. She told me this and asked me why I thought no one liked her. My first reaction was to deny this and reassure her, but it was not what she needed to hear. I tried, with sensitivity, to tell her what I thought the problem was. She thanked me with genuine sincerity and said she would think about this and try to change.

I can remember my mother's behaviour when someone 'important' came to call – the doctor, the vicar, a teacher, or my father's accountant. She would suddenly go mad, cleaning and polishing, as if we weren't all right the way we normally lived.

Even if you were lying prostrate, the sheets had to be changed and every crease removed before the doctor arrived to take your temperature, pat you on the head, and write out a prescription. Then, turning to mother, he would tell her she was doing a wonderful job. I was always convinced he would never have noticed the dust or the evidence of bread and milk slopped on the sheet. I remember on one occasion being dragged out of bed seconds before the bell rang to have clean pyjamas pulled on. But that's the way it was – we all had to conform to mother's idea of what she believed these people expected of us.

Setting Yourself Free from Illusions

To set yourself free from illusions, look at all the things that make you feel good about yourself, where no manipulation, connivance, suppression or denial is involved. Think about those things that allow you to feel completely happy, peaceful and free.

Use your imagination to picture yourself experiencing the difference when you speak without fear, act without worrying about the consequences, enjoy without experiencing guilt, accept success knowing that you deserve it. If it feels good, pursue it. If it doesn't, rethink the situation.

Illusions seem like essential lies. You no longer need them – not if you are going to dare to be yourself.

Avoidance

When a man cannot cope with family life he may spend more and more time at work. He believes that in this way he is doing well and that everything is fine. He fails to see that by using avoidance he is living under the illusion that everything is all right.

A man I know whose relationship went wrong, spent eight hours a day running, swimming and training in the gym. He said he got by this way and felt fine. Instead of using the experience to learn and reach out for a better understanding of himself and how he functioned in a relationship, he escaped into something that prevented him from facing the reality.

We all do this from time to time. Often it is harmless and takes only a little insight to see that it doesn't work. Being overdrawn may result in you not opening letters from your bank (if you don't look you don't know and so for a while may avoid the reality), but the situation will not resolve itself until you face it and do something about it.

You can't be happy while you are hiding behind an illusion and avoiding dealing with the reality of a situation.

Where health is concerned, many people hide from the truth, hoping that if they ignore the signs, the problem will resolve itself. Finding a lump in part of your body and denying the possibility that it may be malignant, won't make it go away. Pretending that you are all right can only put off the moment of truth, and the delay can cause irreparable damage.

Avoiding things does not make them go away. Avoiding the truth about ourselves and others will not change anything. The only way to freedom is by facing reality and dealing with things honestly. Truth can only destroy illusions, it cannot destroy you.

5

Daring to be Yourself

The only thing that prevents us from expressing ourselves freely is fear, and blaming things on someone else is often used as our excuse. Of course things that have happened in the past do have an effect on us; once we recognize why we behave or respond in certain ways, we can start to do something about it. We are no longer trapped or helpless – we do have a choice. When we realize this, we can release ourselves from past traumas and conditioning. It is not change that is so painful, but resistance to it.

When you take full responsibility for your own responses and feelings, you set yourself free to turn daring thoughts into a new way of living. To move forward, you have to set yourself free from self-imposed restrictions.

Facing the fears in you is part of daring to be yourself. It isn't going to be easy. You won't feel comfortable at first. From time to time you may doubt that it can work. But ultimately you will have such an enriched life, filled with joy and love, success and friends, that you will wonder why you ever waited so long.

Step by step you are going to break the chains that bind you and set yourself free. This is essential if you are going to make room in your life for something infinitely better.

Why do you want to make this change in your life, to dare to be yourself? The answer must lie in a sense of disappointment with what you have, or the way in which you perceive yourself, or in the belief that there is much more available to you. There may be a feeling of incompleteness, a reaching out for something that holds more meaning for you.

Daring to be yourself means that you no longer have to struggle to maintain the illusions, that you no longer need to protect yourself from hurt.

You can grow to feel good about who you are, and to live in the knowledge that what you have to offer to the world is unique and you alone can give it.

There are certain laws that rule our world. One is that you cannot remove something without it being replaced by something else. This does not always become immediately apparent. We are often so involved in bemoaning our loss that we fail to see what is awaiting us. Certainly when we let fear out, love is there waiting to move in.

We are taught that pride is a sin, that we must make little of our own accomplishments. However, there is a great difference between pride and vanity. I would like to suggest that you see your talents and accomplishments as a gift. Honour and respect them as you would in another and you will never misuse or abuse them. This does mean that you have to learn to accept genuine compliments graciously. It also means learning to assess honestly your natural gifts and talents and to do away with false modesty.

Comments such as *Oh, I'm really no good at it*, or *It's nothing, anybody could have done it*, when you have just produced a lovely piece of embroidery, made a piece of furniture, or very competently redecorated a room, is actually a rudeness. You are suggesting that the person who offers the praise or compliment doesn't know what they are talking about.

If you are ever going to be yourself, you have to learn

to like who you are and allow your natural gifts to develop.

It is time to take a look at who you think you are. List all the qualities about yourself of which you can feel justly proud. However small, add it to your list, it may turn out to be your biggest asset. Think of the things people have said about you from time to time that you have previously brushed aside from a sense of modesty or disbelief.

Your list should include personal qualities, such as being a good listener, honest, fond of animals, as well as your ability perhaps to service a car engine, use a computer, knit a pullover. Yes! I do mean *everything* you feel you do well. Include also those things you enjoy doing. Allow yourself a few minutes to look at this list and feel good about yourself.

You are now going to list those things about yourself you want to change or to let go. They could include some of the following.

If you find yourself lying to make people feel better about themselves and this makes you uncomfortable, it has to go.

If you behave like a dogsbody to everyone to keep the peace, you are going to have to let go of the fear of their reactions in order to be yourself. You have to love them enough to tell them the truth and, for their own good, help them to make the necessary adjustments in the way they see you. Having made this stand, it is up to you to see that they take on a fair share of the chores.

If you have been used to dressing and playing a part for gain or approval, you are going to have to like yourself sufficiently *as you are*, to change that image. Sometimes we 'dress down' in order not to compete, or to make others feel good. Sometimes we dress in a way to impress. Doing something to impress may be good for business and provided it does not harm you personally, it is acceptable – even necessary – in some circumstances. There is nothing wrong with wanting to dress up. When we first meet people the impression we give will depend on how we present ourselves – it is the intention behind the way we present ourselves, that needs consideration.

If you have been in the habit of humbling yourself in the hope that you will not be challenged or have burdens placed upon you, this also needs to be looked at. *I couldn't possibly – I'm no good at that – You do it so much better than me* – and many other similar self-deprecating statements, are denying your true worth.

Fear is not more real than love, neither is it more powerful – unless you allow it to be so. To believe it, is to make it happen. If you do not allow yourself to believe in your own worth it will go unnoticed. You will fail to see how much you have to offer and how much is waiting for you to grasp.

Where you need to love yourself more in order to have

Your patience may not be obvious when dealing with old people.

the courage to reveal yourself, begin by focusing upon those qualities you admire and find in others: patience, gentleness, kindness, determination, assertiveness, tenacity, courage. By now you are probably thinking that you have none of these qualities. May I assure you that you have – you have just been looking in the wrong place. Having identified them, look for them in yourself.

Your patience may not be obvious when dealing with old people, for instance, but you may show infinite patience when working in the garden or out fishing. You may think you totally lack the ability to be assertive, but there will have been moments when, perhaps for the sake of a child's health, or where safety on the road was concerned, you have been very assertive. (I remember when I was much younger I found it extremely difficult to ask to use someone's toilet, but when I had children I found no difficulty at all in asking on their behalf).

A young man I know told me that he believed he has no right to be assertive. 'You don't know the other person's problems,' he says, 'and so it's wrong to put pressure on them.' When, however, his cattle were in need of fresh supplies of food and they did not arrive, he eventually got on the telephone and was very assertive indeed. He cared enough about the animals to put them first.

The lesson we can learn from this is that if we care enough about something, we will and can assert ourselves. It also proves we have the ability to do so. With a bit of training we can learn to use assertiveness for ourselves where it is necessary.

When you allow other people to push you around what you are saying is that you don't value yourself, and that does your self-image no good at all.

Somewhere inside you there may dwell a longing to be different – tend it with infinite care. Daring to set yourself free from those bonds that have tied you to old behaviour patterns enables you to realize your potential. Everyone whose life touches yours will benefit from this.

You need not worry or fear those things that have happened in the past – they are history. We cannot change history, but if we are wise we may learn from it. Whatever you did or left undone, whatever errors or omissions were made, they cannot prevent you from fulfilling your role in the present or in the future.

A man who has been in prison will be prevented from joining the police force, but the motivation behind the desire to 'put right' or help to enforce law and order can be attained in other areas. He may volunteer to help with young would-be criminals, and through his experiences and present example help to lead the youngsters along a better road.

It takes courage to change direction and to stop doing something that you have been doing for a long time, but courage is within all of us – we only need to recognize it and allow it to emerge. If your desire to dare to be yourself is strong enough, you will be surprised how your courage will come to the rescue.

Many people think that if their circumstances were to change, if they could be given a fresh chance in life, *then* they could change: a new house, new job, new partner, new friends, money – all, or perhaps just one of these, would allow them to start again. If things change externally they believe they will change internally.

The truth is that we cannot escape ourselves or our thoughts – we carry our past around with us until we decide to let it go. We may succeed in temporarily pushing hurtful thoughts and feelings to the inner recesses of the mind, but they will instantly surface when certain stimuli are applied.

Being able to admit mistakes is a mark of maturity. It does not indicate weakness or inadequacy. All too often what we argue about so vehemently is only our opinion or point of view. From where someone else is standing

Daring to be Yourself 55

things may look very different. No one is right or wrong, they are simply seeing things differently.

Why must we always be right? The need to be right is the cause of so many arguments – it is the touch-paper that ignites anger and feelings of resentment. Often the source of the argument is so small, so insignificant that it is of no importance in itself, and yet we insist on being right. Does the name of a place once visited matter so much? Does the date of a certain occasion have to be argued? Is it so terribly important who did what or when? Usually the answer is *No*, and yet we go on arguing the point – hell-bent on being right. Why?

The answer lies in our lack of confidence. We have a deep-rooted need to ensure that our facts or beliefs are accepted, that our opinions are endorsed. Being right makes us feel we are on safe ground. Over and over again it happens, this determination to prove we are right, causing friction and irritability; and this is never more so than within the family. If we could only stand back for a few minutes and ask ourselves 'Is it so important that I am right?' The answer would most often be *No*. Yet there is still that need to convince.

When we need to prove things to other people, what we are saying is that we have no values of our own – we need their agreement, approval or endorsement. If you feel okay about who you are and what you have done it is natural to want to share this with others, but you shouldn't need their blessing before it becomes of value.

When we are in harmony with ourselves we can afford to give in for we lose nothing from it. A new kind of understanding emerges and we can allow the other person to have their say. At least some of the time!

Only when one is suffering from a very poor self-image and constantly being shown that one is in the wrong can this yielding become destructive or damaging. If you feel this could happen to you, it is important to understand that the dominant people arguing their position do so because they actually have a problem. If they were sure of who they were they could afford to be wrong sometimes. See their dominance for what it really is and you are no longer reduced by it.

There is no obstacle that cannot be overcome. History is filled with stories of people with terrible disabilities who have achieved their goals. That's all very well, you may say, but how can I push off and go to work in an underdeveloped country, when I have to care for my sick old dad? Of course you *can* – but what is stopping you is a sense of duty or love. You have unconsciously made your decision. In a way, you have already achieved your goal – namely, caring for others.

I have been reading a book about Stephen Hawking – known as the greatest scientist of our time. He weighs no more than 90lbs (41 kg), is completely paralysed, can only speak through a metallic voice system and is unable to lift his head if it falls forward. Each word he writes, via a computer, is done by the tiny movements of two fingers of one hand – it is all the movement he has. Still he dares; his ideas are revolutionary; he has advanced science more than any other living man – *he refuses to give up*.

It makes one realize that many things we see as obstacles are very poor excuses. If you want to do something powerfully enough, you will find a way. If another human being can do it, then so can you.

Take a few minutes off now and think about daring to be yourself. Are you too submissive, unsure, scared, anxious, worried about other people's opinions? Or are you too aggressive, too stubborn, too selfish, too self-opinionated – and has this become a facade beneath which you hide what you see as weakness? Are you afraid of failure and because of this you never dared to pursue your ambitions? What do you think will happen if you reveal your true self? Who do you think you are and what do you want to change?

Now choose just one aspect of your life that you can immediately start to change or actively improve immediately. Let it be something you never dared to do before. Enhance this by doing the following exercise.

Exercise Seven – Daring to be You

1 Close your eyes and relax. Imagine a present situation in your life that you want to change. Make a picture to represent it in your mind.

2 Now erase that picture in any way that feels okay to you and replace it with the new you in that situation. If you do this with love in your heart, caring about your own feelings, wanting to improve the situation and not to destroy anyone else in the process, you will make the right moves and say things in the best possible way. Turn it into a movie and watch what happens. It's your movie so you can change it if you feel the need.

3 Imagine a positive response to 'daring to be you' in this situation. Feel good about it.

4 Quietly make a promise to yourself that you will, from this moment onward, begin to use this positive behaviour.

5 Open your eyes, sit quietly for a few minutes and think about all the good things this new behaviour can bring about.

Note: a) It is very important that you carry this through. Pause and enhance the positive pictures with your imagination whenever you have any doubt or are tempted to slide back into your old ways. This new behaviour is the beginning of the rest of your life. You are setting a

Pause and enhance the pictures with your imagination.

pattern by making this one change that will help to build your future. Once you discover how well it works, you will be encouraged to adopt more and more positive steps towards your emergence from the chrysalis as a butterfly.

b) Not every response will be positive when you begin to change. People don't like their illusions or facade shattered; most are reluctant to change. They don't like to confront their true selves, and some of your new behaviour is going to make them do just that. They will reject what you are, rather than facing the truth about themselves, even though, for their own sake, they *need* to face that truth. Where they will not accept change in you and react against it, stand firm, know that you have the right to express yourself honestly. You may even be surprised to discover that you can feel compassion for the person who is not yet ready to make or accept changes.

The more confident you become, the easier it will be to follow your heart and to express yourself in words and deeds. Confidence is like a key, it opens so many new doors. Whatever reasons you may believe you have for feeling bad about yourself, know that you can change. Whenever you find that you are putting yourself down, *stop it*.

Start regularly using positive declarations of affirmation. There are books which list these by the hundreds, but you only need perhaps half a dozen at the most. Make sure that they contain very *positive* phrases that leave no room for doubt or manoeuvre in your mind. This means that you avoid phrases like *I will not allow people to put on me*. The mind here can immediately begin to think *So I let people do this to me*.

May I suggest you consider using the following, or similar, affirmations. Use them regularly and, whenever doubt creeps in, use them again and again:

- I can do anything I set out to do.

- I can achieve my goal.

- I can let go and experience total freedom.

- I need only to be myself and I like who I am.

Remember, no more telling yourself you can't. *Can't* is to become obsolete in your vocabulary when you think of yourself. If you tell yourself you *can* just a quarter of the times you have told yourself in the past that you *can't*, you will succeed with flying colours.

6

Daring to Tell the Truth

Now here *is* a challenge. I wonder how many of us could honestly say that we always tell the truth? I suspect there are very few, for most of us are too afraid of upsetting people, shattering their illusions, arousing angry responses, or being rejected.

Most relationships would flounder, if not collapse completely, were total truth to be expressed. How can you tell your partner that you don't like the way she or he speaks to you in certain situations, makes love, or sometimes touches you? If you don't, you are living a lie, and it goes on getting bigger and bigger until you lose sight completely of who you are or what you both want and need from the relationship.

There are ways of putting things right, but some illusions are going to be shattered in the process. Wouldn't that be worth it though, if your relationship became one that is completely free from fear?

All lies are founded on fear. They start in our childhood – if we tell the truth we are likely to be punished, reprimanded, or earn disapproval for some misdeed or omission, and so we avoid the truth or deliberately lie. This progresses in size and emphasis depending on how much we feel we stand to lose by telling the truth.

Children often lie in an endeavour to please. 'How are you getting on with maths?' may be met with 'Okay, no problem'. When the school report arrives, the child who has consistently lied may feel compelled now to hide the report to avoid disappointment or punishment. Thus a behaviour pattern develops.

Some people become so good at telling others what they want to hear that they no longer recognize that they are lying. If you are ever going to be true to yourself, this bolstering of other people's egos has to stop. Here are some of the everyday lies we are all guilty of using from time to time:

How do I look? (He has grown a straggly beard and looks 20 years older.) *You look great!*

Do you want to come with me? (It's pouring with rain and the last thing you want to do is go out.) *Of course!*

Do you like it? (They have painted the lounge deep purple.) *I think it's lovely.*

My children are behaving abominably (They have deliberately poured orange juice on your settee.) *No they're not, they are really sweet.*

Do you like dogs? (Their labrador has just placed two muddy paws on your shirt.) *Yes.*

You're sure it's no bother? (You have about 500 other jobs waiting to be done.) *None at all.*

How do you feel? (You have had a heart attack and just returned from hospital.) *I'm fine!*

You may consider these questions and responses harmless, and if they make the other person feel happy or satisfied does it really matter? The answer is 'no', if you are honestly content with your own feelings in the matter. Be aware, though, that in many cases you are supporting an illusion that prevents the other person from growing.

However, if you find that you are despising yourself for saying such things, or that you feel resentment in having to make such responses, it is time perhaps that you looked at ways to change. Also, if you go on to negate what you have said by talking to someone else about it, you are not being true to yourself or to the person concerned. For example, if you say of a friend, *She's put on at least two stone, but I could never tell her* ... what do you think you are doing? Are you helping or deceiving?

There are times when our actions deny the truth. If we don't exactly use words then it seems okay, but people aren't usually that stupid – unless they are totally blinded by their own illusions they *see* what we are saying in other ways. When we act out a lie, sooner or later it becomes apparent. If you say you like someone else's children but always avoid asking them to tea when they have the children with them, they'll eventually get the message.

You may feel selfish in wanting things your own way. When you voice a dislike or say when you don't want to do something, or go somewhere, it will always be a decision you have to make depending on how important it is to you. If you decide to do something anyway, then decide also to enjoy it. Go with positive intentions. Simmering resentment or guilt does no one any good.

You may be able to recall a time when you did something to please someone else though you didn't really want to, and enjoyed yourself enormously. Look for something to enjoy in all experiences – the smell of freshly baked bread when you have to do the shopping, the benefit to your complexion when you are forced to walk in the rain, holding a really worthwhile conversation when you have to go to a cocktail party. We can learn from every experience when our minds and hearts are open.

Clients often tell me that they would like to change and to express their feelings but are convinced their partner couldn't cope with this. I ask them if they perhaps underestimate the strength of feelings, the depth of love? However, the next frightening thought that has to be faced is whether the relationship is worth it if a couple cannot be honest with each other?

If you were doing something that offends or actually puts off your partner, wouldn't you want to know so that you could put it right? This must be seen as communication prompted by the desire to have a richer, deeper relationship, not as criticism. It is not going to help if you suddenly announce: 'I can't stand you doing that to me.' Imagine the reaction: 'You could have told me before! You have just been making a fool of me – pretending to like it.'

Perhaps the following approach would be more constructive: 'As I've grown older I've changed, some things affect me differently now. When you do . . . I feel . . .' And then you give a positive alternative that can benefit both of you: 'I do love it though when you . . .'

Take another example. You are always being put down by someone in the office in front of others. For months you have longed to tell the culprit but feared the fuss or possible reprisal. However, it is making you miserable, affecting your work, and it's time you told the truth. 'John,' you say, 'I know you only think it a bit of fun, but when you speak to me like that in front of others, you really hurt me, and I would rather you didn't do it.' Now he may say you are being too sensitive, or he didn't mean anything by it, but he'll know, deep down inside, that he shouldn't continue. If he does, speak right out and tell him again that you don't like it and that it hurts.

We are often asked for our opinion, sometimes about something simple like a new tie or dress – or it could be about a child. How often have we avoided the truth when the truth is what people really need to hear. If a dress makes your friend look 20 years older or two stone heavier, wouldn't it be kinder to say it doesn't, in your opinion, do her justice? And if a child is rude or badly behaved, maybe telling its parents the truth will give them the courage to do something about it.

Criticism is often misinterpreted: if you criticize it can be taken that you don't like or love that person. Where this is happening it needs to be made clear – *I love you, but I don't like what you are doing.*

So often we stay silent or mutter half-truths rather than help the person to a realization that could improve and enrich his or her life. Criticism must never be made maliciously – your intention has to be for good.

Where your opinion is requested, it is, after all, only your opinion. The recipient is free to accept or reject it. You may be pleasantly surprised at the respect this gains you. I know there are people I can ask, trusting them to give me an honest answer, and not just what they think I want to hear. This will need practice. You will be surprised, now that you are aware, how often you have lied or told half-truths, sometimes believing you would hurt or offend, other times because you wanted to be liked.

When the boss comes up with a new idea that he believes will save the company money and you think it will be a disaster, what do you say about it? He asks for your response – he wants your approval. Credit him with the intelligence he has ascribed to you in asking your opinion and tell him the truth. If you don't believe it will work you are not doing anyone a favour by lying. When you are standing in the dole queue, it isn't going to help to turn to him and say, 'I never thought for one moment that crazy idea of yours would work.'

The only time I ever lied to my father was when his cancer was diagnosed. We thought he could not cope with the truth about his illness. Looking back now, I realize that although we acted this way to protect his feelings, we denied ourselves, as well as him, the opportunity to draw closer and to share together what was happening to him.

I am convinced that during those last few days he did know but said nothing, believing we could not handle his awareness, and so we all acted an artificial role.

Intentions

How often do we delude ourselves by believing our intentions are different from what they really are?

You write a loving letter to one of your children telling them how you miss them when what you are actually saying is *It's about time you paid us a visit*.

You assure someone you want to help when what you really want is to be seen helping.

You declare that you want to become more assertive to improve on your job, when what you really want is to get back at the boss.

You tell people you want them to come and enjoy the garden when what you really want is their praise.

With most of these no harm is done, except you are acting a lie and preventing yourself from living your life at a higher level. However, there are situations where you need to be very certain of your underlying intention, otherwise you can find yourself in deep trouble.

Learning to be attentive to your true intentions gives you a sensitivity that opens up your life. You can be open with everyone, there is no fear of being exposed. You know exactly who you are and why you are doing what you are doing. No one can ever destroy your integrity or detract from it.

Even the law recognizes that intention is often of more importance than the act. It describes the difference between murder and manslaughter.

Be honest with yourself and examine your intentions. You will be amazed at how different they are from how you had seen them on a superficial level. Obviously you cannot do this with every act, or every sentence you utter. But by making yourself aware of your intention, very soon this new attitude will become so much a part of you, that you automatically become attuned to your inner self and intentions.

Sometimes we are guilty of telling ourselves that we act out of love, when in truth it is to keep the peace, or out of a sense of duty or obligation. In such cases it will not get the same positive response – at least not deep down inside where it truly matters. Some people who profess love for another have a deep-down need to possess or control. This is not love. Love sets you free and is a wonderful expression of sharing and caring; it does not manipulate, intimidate or seek to dominate.

Telling the truth with a sense of caring can never cause any real damage. It may not always be easily accepted, but you will be able to live with yourself and gain a new sense of respect for who you are.

When you speak the truth you credit the other person with integrity.

7

Dare to Love

The reason most of us lose out on love is that we dare not love with all our hearts. We are afraid of rejection, afraid lest someone uses it against us, afraid of being hurt.

Whether our love is for friends, parents, partners, or even children, there is often an underlying need to protect ourselves.

If we are lucky, we may once have loved completely. Now it may have come to an end. Still we are lucky because we at least had the experience of total loving. To have loved and lost is not the end of the world. We know how, and if we choose to remember all that was good in that experience, we will be open to love the next time.

It is often easier to love pets than people – they won't let you down, they won't go off with someone else, they won't decide to move away or go to live in Australia. We create an illusion that the dog, cat, gerbil, loves us totally in return. This isn't possible. Animals cannot experience human emotions, but in their own way they may exhibit loyalty and affection, and they fulfil a need for companionship. The relationship with the pet offers no threat, but it is very different from daring to love another human being with all the risks and joyful communication that can take place.

Many of us are in love with an idea (or ideal) and mistake it for the real thing. Clients who have lost a partner to someone else and are struggling to come to terms with this talk to me about their feelings. They feel their trust has been betrayed. They declare that they are still in love with the person involved and that they cannot live without him/her. Then they go on to describe how cruel, thoughtless, manipulative, heartless, the partner has proven to be. I ask if they can truly love such a person as they have just described. There is a pause, and sometimes, if they are able, they realize what they have been saying. 'He (or she) wasn't always like that,' they say defensively. 'It's all the fault of the other person, they have made him (or her) like that.'

They are actually in love with the beliefs they had about the man or woman. The way they originally perceived their partner is what they are in love with. They still have a need to hold on to the illusion. Until they are able to let go of this and look at the truth, they cannot move on.

All too often we idolize a dream, an illusion that we have created around the person upon whom we latch our feelings. Later, after the illusion is shattered, we may find ourselves saying, 'We were never really suited' or 'We had nothing in common'. At the time, though, we could see nothing of this; we wanted or needed to love somebody and they happened to be there.

Ideally, loving is a two-way thing. For this to happen, we have to allow love into our hearts. We have to dare to let go of all our defences. Men often find it much harder to experience this emotion than women. They put it down to 'being soft' or see it as a weakness; they are often embarrassed to admit to such feelings.

It can sometimes take a tragedy to release feelings and expressions of love. The near-death of a child or partner, the risk of losing a loved one to someone else, a debilitating illness that makes one person vulnerable, can all offer the relationship a new depth of meaning. How sad it is, though, to think that someone has to nearly die before his or her partner can confess to loving feelings.

To receive love is a bit like accepting a compliment, whereas so many people sweep it away as if it was something to fear. They fail to perceive it as a gift. What they are really saying is, *I'm not worthy of it; how can you love a person like me?*

Fortunately for all of us, we are born to be loved. Most of us will have had the loving care of a mother during our early formative years – we did nothing to earn it. In fact, we probably kept them awake at nights, vomited over their clothes and caused mountains of washing. It made no difference; they just kept on loving us.

As I said earlier, love is not conditional. We are all capable of loving and being loved – we do not have to be physically attractive, clever, rich or well educated before someone will love us. Just as we are, there are people to love us. But to gain the rewards we have to break down the barriers – and, yes, even risk being hurt.

Loving, I am convinced, is much more important than being loved, and yet so many people are crying out for someone to love them. The way is so simple: when you love you become lovable. When someone loves us, we see ourselves reflected in their eyes – they raise us up and it makes us want to be better people.

Love is not a cringing pathetic thing that allows the recipients to behave as badly as they please. Neither should love reduce you to a mindless idiot devoid of your own opinions or ideas. Love is a powerful, magnificent force; it is tender and constant; love is respecting and accepting; love has no barriers and no conditions.

To fully experience loving you have to take that leap into the unknown. You don't know how your love will be received. But if the feelings are selfless, and if you truly want to bring joy and happiness to the other person, you have to dare to give your love unconditionally.

If someone cannot accept your love, you have not failed, they are simply not yet ready for such commitment – they are not ready for you. Take heart, there are many people out there in the world desperately searching for a love like yours.

When you look upon your family, friends and colleagues with real love in your heart, forgiveness comes easily. You find yourself understanding the person behind the act of thoughtlessness, or of fear, or of greed, and you do not take it personally. They have a problem that has not yet been addressed.

Few people are really wicked or vindictive. Often they will hit out or behave badly because they are hurting inside. Once you begin to understand this, it becomes easy to love them and not take on board their negativity. It is a bit like the little boy who says, 'I hate you, Daddy,' because he is not allowed to do something he wants to do. Daddy doesn't get upset; he understands the feelings behind the words and will often reward such words with a hug and say, 'Never mind, we'll find something else to do.'

You have to take that leap into the unknown.

True love is strong and firm, not weak and indulgent. The mother who gives in to the child again and again is not demonstrating love, but encouraging weakness of character. We all know that a badly behaved child is not welcomed and only the deluded relatives continue to think how lovely he/she is. A parent's role must be to teach total independence, to provide security, love and stability. That does not mean becoming a slave to the family. Saying no can mean *I care, and because I love you I have to deny you this*.

Compassion, understanding and love are easier to handle than hate, anger or frustration. They feel a lot better too! In almost all cases it is better to act than to react. Gradually a change of heart takes place and the nasty old emotions are experienced less and less. The world begins to look a better place.

Where anger is one of our most destructive emotions, love is one of our most constructive. The act of loving can communicate more than a thousand words – it can change the world. Sadly, we so often misuse love. We call what we feel 'love', and then use its guise as a powerful manipulator. This is one of the very worst ways of taking something very precious and misusing it.

When I hear angry frustrated mothers yelling at their children in the street I want to stop them and say, 'Try loving him instead, it will feel a lot better.' *Perhaps one day I will dare to do so*.

I saw an example of this loving approach in action recently. A couple with a stacked trolley were standing behind me in the supermarket queue. Balanced on top was a small boy who was obviously bored. He was making quite a lot of noise – he wanted attention. The mother's voice rose higher and higher as she became more and more exasperated. Suddenly the father rubbed his hand through the boy's hair and tickled him under the chin. The whine turned to giggles. They began a game that said *I love you*. I walked away with a warm glow in my heart.

I was once asked to visit a man who was dying of cancer. His wife met me at the doorstep and ushered me into a delightful room with french windows opening out onto a garden filled with colour and cool green trees. The man (I'll call him Michael) was lying on a bed that had been brought downstairs so that he could look out at the beautiful view. His wife told me she recorded stories and things of interest from the radio in order that he might listen to these at night when sleep eluded him.

I found Michael a gentle, charming man. I also perceived at once that he was very, very ill. We talked together for a little while and I then made him a tape recording to try and help reduce his awareness of pain by directing his thoughts back to happy memories. Afterwards, his wife, Connie, asked me into the kitchen. Michael had already drifted into a light sleep and no longer needed me. She then burst into tears. I thought at first it was because of the seriousness of her husband's condition, but it wasn't. In a broken voice she told me the problem was that she didn't love him. This made her feel terribly guilty and the guilt was worse than all the things she had to bear in supporting and caring for him during this time. The more I listened, the more I knew that Connie was wrong. Finally I said, 'You do love him. You could never do all these things for him if you didn't. You would not be considering him every minute of every day if you did not love him. You would not have agreed to nurse him at home, if you didn't love him.' 'Then why do I feel like this?' she asked. Because Connie no longer felt any physical desire for him, she thought she no longer loved him. I tried to explain that this was often the case. Behind all that is civilized, we are still animals, and animals usually withdraw from one that is dying. I assured her that under the circumstances it was perfectly okay for her to have these physical feelings of rejection.

On my next visit I saw that Connie had changed. She

was sitting beside Michael holding his hand, and when we left the room she bent and kissed him. There was such tenderness in that kiss that I wanted to weep. Connie had discovered that there was a vast difference between physical loving and fulfilling an emotional need.

I am not using this story to suggest that love and sex are separate, or that one does not compliment the other, but if sex was an essential part of loving between man and woman, how would we fare in illness, old age, or disability?

Quite recently I found myself sitting next to a gentleman on a long plane journey. He struck up a conversation concerning values. Soon he was telling me of his niece whom he had helped bring up. Every week, he told me, he used to fetch her home from school and sit with her while she did her homework. Over the years he had tried to influence her with his ideals and standards of behaviour that he believed would be for her own good. Only now she was grown and out in the world, and to his immense disappointment he saw that she was violating his beliefs and values.

The niece was currently in hospital and quite seriously ill. He found that he could not visit her. 'I'm thinking of cutting her out of my life completely,' he said. 'I don't think I can ever forgive her for the way she has behaved.' He was obviously deeply distressed. 'Do you love her?' I asked. He took several minutes to answer. 'I don't know,' he finally replied. 'I don't see how I can after what she has done.'

I suggested that perhaps it was his pride that was hurt because she had, by her very actions, rejected his values. He agreed that this could be so. 'Why not visit her,' I suggested. 'Tell her how much you care about her. You can tell her you don't approve or condone what she has done, but that doesn't stop you loving her.'

He was silent for the rest of the journey and I respected

this and returned to my book. As I rose to leave the plane he held out his hand. 'I was meant to meet you,' he said. 'Thank you.' We smiled and parted company and I knew what he intended to do. He had been making his love conditional on the niece behaving to his set of values and it hadn't worked.

I sometimes think that part of teenage rebellion is a way of testing our love. Of course most teenagers need to rebel, it is part of the 'breaking away' that must take place. It is often accompanied by a lot of guilt that is only made worse if the parents show how much they are hurt.

From my own experiences and observations I find that if there is a strong foundation of love to the relationship, the rebellion rarely goes too far and does nothing to destroy the mature relationship that will eventually develop.

Loving enough to let go, loving enough to trust your children, loving enough to believe that things will work out – all these positive feelings will help you to survive the traumas of bringing up a family. Their defiance or rejection of your values is not a rejection of your love or of you, but as they grow towards independence they need to do things their way, however painful for you.

Sometimes we need to express our fears in order that the child can reassure us. When my youngest son was about to go off to university I was extremely worried by the thought that he might get caught up in experimenting with drugs. I told him how I felt. 'But Mum,' he said, 'I've never even smoked a cigarette. Don't you think I am capable of saying no to drugs.' It was the reassurance I needed. My fear had clouded my love – I should have known better. I needed, however, to express my fear.

There are some people who feel compelled to keep putting love to the test. They abuse, misuse, cheat, trick – they cannot believe they are loved and often end up driving away the one who is of real value to them.

When you love someone, it doesn't mean you have to

put up with being badly treated, and you shouldn't be put in the position of having to constantly behave in a convincing manner because your partner finds it hard to accept your love and trust in it.

Remember that you cannot hug unless you open your arms. We have to let love in. Love sets you free. Love casts out all fear. Love is the finest emotion you will ever dare to express.

8

Expressing Emotions

We spend far more time in suppressing or denying emotions than in expressing them. This is strange when you think about it, for every emotion has a special purpose and value.

Grief is a powerful emotion we try hard to hide. If you have ever been to a funeral in the Western world, you will have observed close relatives and friends all trying desperately to behave as if they are not bereft. And yet this feeling in itself is an honour to the one who has died. It is also therapeutic. We need to express the emotion of grief; we need to say I'm hurting.

The problem is that we are afraid of our emotions. We are afraid of losing control, or of being seen to lose control. We may be afraid that expression of our emotions will be used against us. We fear disapproval and rejection; we are afraid of being misunderstood. We see our emotions as a revelation of our vulnerability.

Genuine gut feelings have such an important function that we ought to be aware of them and to know how to read them.

Feelings are much nearer expressions of truth than words can ever be. *I'm really happy for you* has no meaning unless you give some indication of emotion behind the words. *This really frightens me* carries much more weight if there is an expression of fear in your eyes – and you are much more likely to be taken seriously.

Have you ever witnessed someone hurt themselves and heard people laugh at the same time as saying they were sorry? It may have looked funny, but I bet the person who was hurt didn't believe that the onlooker was caring very much about how he felt.

One of the most frightening things is the realization that our emotions are controlling us and running our lives. On the other hand, if we are in control of our emotions we can use them instead of being used *by* them. In this way they can powerfully help us to achieve what we have to do or wish to do with our lives. Choosing to use your emotions instead of being run by them starts with conscious choice. Most people run around like chickens with their heads tucked under one wing – you have to lift your head and confront the truth.

Stress *can* be turned into motivation. Fear *can* help us stay alive. Guilt *can* help us to see how we could do things differently next time.

Expressing emotions can work as an outlet, a release of tension. It is a way of telling someone what we are feeling.

Anger is a most powerful and destructive emotion. More often than not, anger is a response to a feeling that we have been badly treated. Viewed constructively, this serves to tell us that we need to work on building our sense of self-worth. When you absolutely *know* that you are not like that, or never had such an intention, then you no longer have the need to react. The feelings have still been useful if we learn from them.

If you are still hurting, communicate – dare to tell the person or persons involved how you are feeling and, most important of all, *why*.

Anger ought not to be a hitting out because you are

feeling mistreated in some way. But it is a very useful signal if read correctly. The following story illustrates that it is not easy to express or interpret anger, even in a simple, everyday situation.

Mother has spent most of the morning in the kitchen preparing a splendid lunch. She calls the family in. No one comes. The children continue their game and the husband wants to finish planting his row of cabbages. The minutes tick past. She calls again. The meal is spoiling by being kept warm in the oven. Half an hour later everyone rolls casually into the kitchen. By now she is feeling furious. She is not angry over the meal spoiling, although that is what she says. The anger is because no respect or consideration has been given to the effort she has put into something for them. The real problem is that she feels no one cares about her efforts or feelings – that she is of no worth. If she could express this, the family would most probably admit to being thoughtless and selfish and tell her that they hadn't realized how important this was to her, and her sense of worth would stay intact.

Most of us are not clairvoyant, we need to be told. The closer we are to someone, the less we notice everyday behaviour. Accepting the way you are can be a compliment, being taken for granted can be infuriating.

Anger, frustration, envy, jealousy, guilt and fear can all be used constructively if we pause and ask ourselves *Why am I feeling like this?* You need to be honest with your answer and then to deal with the core of the problem.

Let's do a little experiment.

Exercise Eight – Expressing Emotion

1 Close your eyes and for a few minutes think about an emotion that you don't enjoy. Remember when you last

had that feeling. Perhaps it is still with you because you have never found a satisfactory way of dealing with it.

2 Now ask yourself, 'Why am I having this feeling?' Is it because you feel offended? Do you feel ignored? Misunderstood? Has someone been rejecting you in some way? Perhaps you feel resentful because you are taken for granted.

3 Imagine now that you express this emotion. Go to the person or persons involved and tell them that you are feeling hurt, angry or whatever. You need a response not a reaction. You want them to help you change the way you feel and in order to do this you have to express and deal with that emotion. Picture the way in which this could be resolved.

4 Observe how you feel.

The next step has to be taken for real. You have to dare to follow this through and actually do it. Go through this exercise several times first if you are having difficulty in putting it into action. Build positive pictures in your mind that help to propel you forward.

The following stories show how the above exercise can resolve two different anger problems.

In the first, Elizabeth feels that her mother-in-law is always critical of her. She thinks that she disapproves of the way she is bringing up her children. She knows that her mother-in-law has said some critical things about her to other members of the family. Elizabeth is feeling very angry inside. When, however, the mother-in-law visits, Elizabeth is charming and doesn't let any of the anger show. The only person who knows how Elizabeth feels is her husband, John, and he is torn between the two women in his life whom he loves. How can he intervene between them? He feels that it is Elizabeth's problem.

Suppose now that Elizabeth has just done the above exercise. She honestly wants to improve the relationship rather than just tell her mother-in-law what she thinks of her. She decides to put into action her visualization the very next time John's mother calls.

It happens to be a lovely day. The children are outside playing and Elizabeth makes the tea. 'Mum,' she says. 'I need to talk to you. I've been feeling so angry over the way you talk about me and the way you think about me that I have to tell you.' The mother-in-law looks astonished. She always thought she got on well with Elizabeth. She listens in silence as Elizabeth voices her feelings.

'I'm sorry. I never realized,' she responds. 'When you joined our family you became like a daughter to me. I talk about you and sometimes criticize you as if you were my own child – just as you talk to me about your children. It was never meant to hurt. I love you. I would never do anything deliberately to upset you.'

Elizabeth is silent. She doesn't know what to think now. It's true she talks about her children and tells stories against them sometimes. It doesn't mean she doesn't love them or that she isn't infinitely proud of them. Suddenly she sees that it is the same thing. To John's mother she *is* just like a daughter. In fact it is a compliment that her mother-in-law feels she can say these things. In a flash she sees how close it brings them.

'I will try to be more careful,' John's mother says. 'I do speak out of turn on occasions.' They smile and sip their tea. Suddenly there isn't a problem at all. It feels good to be loved and to have been able to express their feelings.

The second example, a true story, concerns Evan, who had applied for the tenancy of a country inn. He was sure he could improve on the trade. He was inventive, hard working and positive. He was also used to managing people and money. After a very successful interview he was pretty sure he would get the pub. Imagine his disappointment when a letter arrived a few days later telling him that it had been offered to someone else.

Evan's disappointment turned to anger. They interviewer had misled him. There had been so many signs that he was just the man they were looking for that he couldn't believe they had actually turned him down. He got out a writing pad. He was, by this time, fuming. Having nicely licked the flames into an inferno, he was going to tell the company exactly what he thought of them.

Then something happened inside him. Evan began to think that if they really wanted the best man for the job, then they must have chosen the other fellow truly believing he could best fill the post. No one was having a go at Evan; no one was trying to put him down. For whatever reason, they believed the other man was right for the job.

Evan wrote a letter thanking them for their courtesy in letting him know. He said how disappointed he was, but understood that they had selected the man they believed could best run that business. He ended by saying he still hoped that there might be a pub for him in the future. Evan was offered the very next pub that became vacant.

Having honestly looked at his feelings, dealt with the angry response that followed the rejection, he had then dared to express himself. He had investigated his feelings, made the necessary changes, and was still able to write and tell them of his disappointment.

Feelings are much better expressed than denied. However, we do need to look at our intention so that what comes out is a sincere desire to do something positive about the situation and not just an angry retaliation because we are hurting.

It's okay to say 'I'm feeling angry, or upset, or hurt,' and then, 'I need to talk about it.' If the response is one of refusal or even denial – for many people do back off from any display of emotion – then tell them, 'This is important to me.' Even this may not always get the listening ear you need. You then have to make choices.

- You can talk to someone else – and we often do this, we use another person to whom we express our feelings. This doesn't get the same result but it helps.

- You try another approach.

- You decide it isn't that important, but at least it's your decision and you stay in control.

- You may, in some cases, need to take professional advice or legal action.

For example, you may experience problems with noisy neighbours. After repeated requests have made no difference, you may feel the need for outside intervention – and here you could choose to consult a solicitor. Or, if you have become so upset by your partner's behaviour that you feel you cannot go on in that relationship, you could go to an organization such as Relate.

Experiencing Happiness

We ought to find time to experience and express such a positive feeling as happiness, but many times such feelings are ignored or go unnoticed. Happiness, joy, having fun, are all so beneficial that we need to cultivate them. We need to give them room to expand and to play a larger part in our life.

People can forget how to be happy. They become so bowed down with what they see as their problems or responsibilities that they lose touch with one of the emotions that could actually help. Being happy is therapeutic. Happiness is healing.

Even as I was writing this book I received a phone call from an elderly gentleman whom I visited earlier during the week. It had been a number of years since we last met and it was only his ill health that finally prompted me to make the journey. 'Your visit has done me more good than a thousand pills,' he said. I knew he meant it. When I first saw him he had looked grey, sickly, and totally lacking in energy. When we parted, his eyes were bright, he hugged me with strength back in his arms, he appeared relaxed and at peace. *He was happy*.

I would like to share with you a personal experience of happiness. It happened early one morning when I was out riding my pony. Because of family circumstances, I had to try and exercise the pony before my husband went to work. The older children could get themselves out of bed, dress and have breakfast, but the youngest one had to come with me.

So there I was on this lovely spring morning, trotting down the lane with my little boy sitting astride the saddle in front of me. We were experiencing problems due to my husband's ill health; he had been told to give up work if he wanted to live beyond the next couple of years. How we were going to manage and support six children, we didn't yet know. There was certainly plenty to think about, and to worry about, as I trotted down that lane. And yet what I was experiencing was the sunshine on my face, the fresh smells of the countryside, the willingness of the pony, and the little warm body of my son pressed close to mine.

At that moment, I realized I was perfectly happy. The problems hadn't disappeared, they still had to be faced, yet what I was actually doing gave me a deep sense of happiness. At the same time I also realized that happiness isn't a constant state. It is more like tiny jewels in time. We need to be aware of them, to store them away so that they can be taken out from time to time and re-experienced.

Many people are pursuing happiness, believing it to be their goal. But in fact it is only when they give up the pursuit and experience what they have 'now' that they will be able to attain it. Happiness is a state of awareness.

Happiness can be found in the contemplation of a flower, the smell of fresh mown grass, a hug from a friend. Attaining material possessions or recognition does not, of itself, bring deepdown happiness. Reaching your goal may allow you to experience a sense of pride and achievement, but that is not happiness. We may think material gain will bring happiness, but the feeling soon diminishes and we are off again in pursuit of something else to make us happy.

There are many times when we are happy and fail to acknowledge it. Perhaps you have been working in the garden, uninterrupted for a couple of hours. You come in to wash your hands, and as you are doing this you think back and realize that for the past two hours you have been blissfully happy – and it had nothing to do with anyone else.

We are wrong to make our happiness dependent on other people. Happiness has to come from within. It is good to share your feeling with others – but still it comes from you. It is the way you feel. Talk about it – tell people when you feel happy. We all need to hear more good news.

Out walking my dog, I pause to speak with neighbours. We talk about the weather, a house that has recently come on the market, the appalling news on TV. Sometimes, when I'm lucky, they tell me about their happiness. Perhaps a grandchild has arrived in the family, or a child has done something really worthy or just plain funny; someone may have been to a wedding or enjoyed a day out by the sea. Happiness shared is a gift of far more value than anything you can buy in the shops.

When you return from work and your partner asks, 'How did your day go?', do you recount the nice things? Something that made you laugh? A moment when you felt happy? Or do you talk about the difficult customer you had to deal with; problems with the bank manager; losing a colleague to another store?

A friend called on me the other day. He had just dropped his wife off at work. 'As she walked away,' he told me, 'I had this lovely thought – she is a nice person. I am lucky.' He shared his happiness and it stayed with me all day.

There are people who think it wrong to be happy when there is so much misery in the world – so many people suffering, so many wars going on. This is true; there is a terrible waste of life, time, resources and energy being uselessly expended and yet we change nothing by feeling miserable or sad because of it. If we are happy and caring we send out very positive energy that can affect many.

Try each day to find something to do that enables you to experience happiness, however brief. Feel the glow of happiness when a small child's hand creeps into yours, feel happy when someone looks directly at you and smiles. Pause and listen to the life around you and be happy that you can hear and see and smell and reach out and touch something.

Shyness

Trapped by the fear that people will not accept them as they are, shy people avoid contact. They have so much to give, want desperately to be part of things, but cannot cope with the powerful feelings that seem to take over and totally control what they do.

If you are one of those people who become self-conscious or dumb in the company of others, the first step towards freedom is to shift your focus from what you are not *to* what you are. It is important to focus on your good qualities.

Shyness can be learned from our parents. Just as we learn how to hold a knife and fork, make our own bed, speak a language by copying our parents, so we learn how to communicate with others, how to project ourselves, how to give of ourselves by example.

Another cause of shyness may be an unhappy incident at school which has made a child feel isolated and different. Being different results in feeling threatened – the victim loses identity with the group that offers security. A bad experience that separates in this way and creates fear or self-doubt is enough to make a child crawl back into his or her shell – never to emerge fully again.

In a way, shy people are very selfish. By this I do not mean they will not do or give of themselves to others, but that they are so turned in on themselves that their whole focus is on what people are thinking of them or saying about them. The fear is so powerful it can even make people feel ill.

When shy people walk into a room of strangers, or even a group of people they already know, they are so concerned about how they are being seen that they have no energy left to attend to anyone else. They fail to notice other shy people who need someone to talk to or stand next to. They often believe that no one else can be feeling as they do, or suffering as much as they are.

One of the best ways to deal with shyness in a social setting is by caring about others. Find someone who looks as if they need your company. Admitting your feelings of apprehension or shyness will only be met with kindness. Do something, *anything*, that takes your mind away from your own feelings.

Shy people more than almost anyone else want to change. No one can change your self-image for you – but you can!

A very nice lady once brought her son to see me because she was so concerned over the boy's behaviour. He worked on their farm with his father and was good at the job but could not bring himself to help twice a week at their market stall. He felt everyone was looking at him and this made him want to run away and hide. I suggested to Chris that he begin to observe the people who came to the stall – how they approached, the difference between men and women when they enquired about the produce, which ones paid willingly and which ones were reluctant to part with their money. It started off as a kind of game in studying people and what made them tick; it went on to be an interest that he found so absorbing that he completely lost his feelings of self-consciousness. He learned how to look outwards instead of inwards.

Some people who believe they are shy discover that when they talk to someone who has similar interests, they become so enthusiastic they quite forget their shyness. Others only feel self-conscious in certain situations – this is usually when they feel all eyes are on them, or for some reason they become the centre of attention. The truth is that the majority of people do not like to be in the limelight, but there are times when it is going to happen, and to be relaxed is the best way of coping.

Taking a number of very deep breaths does help you to relax – so that's where you start. Then focus on one person – talk to them if you can. Try to see it as a one-to-one situation. Even if you are called upon to address a group of people, talk to one – after all, each person listening is only one person – then they don't become a mass. It just so happens that you have a number of single people each listening to you at the same time. Don't worry about saying the wrong thing or messing things up – people are usually with you if they are listening to you. Those who are deliberately rude have a problem of their own that they need to address, and you don't have to take it on board as if it were your fault. Remember also that you are only human – you don't have to be perfect or superhuman. Say if you feel awkward or nervous, it will always get a warm response. It's the big-heads that people can't stand.

9

Daring to Have Fun

When did you last have fun? You know, the sort of fun you had as a child. Can you remember being taken on a mystery trip and ending up sitting on the wall of a harbour fishing with a line and hook? Or going to a Halloween party where everyone dressed up? Having a midnight feast was fun, wasn't it?

Fun and a sense of humour have many times saved a situation. Have you ever been at loggerheads with someone and then one of you sees the funny side of the situation? The laughter works like magic.

There is nothing wrong with enjoyment and having fun. We don't have to spend our whole lives being seriously sober, worrying about the state of the world. You are not going to become heartless and uncaring by choosing sometimes to enjoy yourself.

Many times we spoil enjoyment with feelings of guilt. *I couldn't, I'd feel guilty*, is a response I often get when I suggest someone takes a break from the children or caring for a elderly relative. Why, for goodness sake? You don't have to be a martyr, and by taking a break you come back to the job or duty refreshed and better equipped to cope.

Enjoying food is another experience spoiled by feelings

of guilt. *I shouldn't be eating this* is one of the craziest things to say. Why shouldn't you? If you are worried about your weight and you honestly believe this is going to make things worse, you don't have to eat it. If you do choose to, then at least enjoy it and cut down on something else. The occasional indulgence thoroughly enjoyed can make it easier to eat sensibly the rest of the time. Scientific research has recently shown that food enjoyed actually puts on less weight than food eaten while experiencing bad feelings. What we think causes a direct chemical response in the body, and enjoying food is now seen to be good for you.

Daring to have fun sometimes means having to handle other people's disapproval. This can be hard when those people are close to you. What they are really saying is that they don't understand how you could be doing this – it doesn't seem right or proper.

Recently in a national newspaper there was a story about a group of elderly people who decided to have a party. They played all the old records that revived feelings of nostalgia. In particular they played Max Bygraves records until a neighbour complained to the police. By the time the police arrived the record had changed. They were gently cautioned. One man of 68 years said, 'We just wanted to let our hair down and have a good time.'

If it had been a regular occurrence I could have sympathized with the neighbour who complained, but it was only that once and they were having such fun. I'd like to think they didn't let the neighbour's disapproval spoil it for them.

Pam and I used to have a day out together each week. We would usually start off by playing squash – badly, but that never bothered either of us as we enjoyed ourselves so much. Then we would explore or visit some place that captured our imaginations.

One day we were in a restaurant in Bath, England and

I was seriously explaining how 'they' had now discovered that all plants had feelings. She watched me dip my spoon into the soup and touched my hand. 'I don't think you had better eat that,' she said. 'Why?' I asked. She pointed to a piece of green leek floating on the top. 'You might hurt its feelings,' she said.

Well, we began to laugh. We laughed until my tears joined the leek in the soup bowl. I imagine every one of the diners must have wondered what was going on. If we had looked around we would probably have seen some frowns of disapproval. When we went to pay the bill Pam apologized for our merriment.

'Don't apologize,' the waitress said. 'We have enjoyed every minute just watching you two.'

It goes to show that sometimes your enjoyment can overflow into other lives. Pam died three years ago, yet still what I remember most about her was her capacity for enjoyment. Just thinking about her makes me smile – I bet she's having fun wherever she is.

'We just wanted to let our hair down and have a good time.'

A sense of humour is a wonderful thing to have. Humour comes in all guises. You may be sitting at a show, stone cold sober, without a glimmer of a smile, next to someone who is roaring with laughter, and you can find nothing funny in it. Then a child says something and you find yourself rolling in your seat with gusts of laughter.

When you find someone with the same sense of humour as yours, you immediately strike up a rapport. It feels as if you have always known each other.

A total lack of humour is one of the saddest things I know. Yet many people hide their capacity to see the funny side of things because they think it unacceptable or childish.

Do you remember the looks from your teacher when something struck you as being funny in class? Some kids have this ability to make the rest of the class laugh – they just can't help it. Fancy giving the class lines or keeping them in during break time because they laughed. If I was a teacher I would give extra marks for laughter and fun. I know my grandchildren learn far better when we make things fun. It doesn't matter whether it's learning to swim or digging the garden – have fun, make a few jokes, laugh aloud, and the job gets done in half the time.

I recall my father's dry humour that was often overlooked by the rest of the family in moments of stress. His humour on the day before he died will stay with me forever. Responding to a distressed phone call from my mother, the doctor arrived at the house. Father had cancer of the stomach and had haemorrhaged badly in the early hours of the morning. 'We'd better have you back in hospital, George,' the doctor said. 'If you need a transfusion or special treatment it can't easily be done at home.'

My father gave his little grin and said, 'If you send me back there much more, they will begin to think I like it.' Then, seeing the look of distress on my young daughter's face, he commented, 'What's wrong with you? You look like a sour peach.' Despite the seriousness of the situation he made us all laugh.

Daring To Be Outrageous

This title may sound rather flippant, but the rewards from being outrageous occasionally can be so beneficial that it seems a shame that they are denied to most of us for fear of shocking or being found lacking.

One evening I went out with a friend by car to watch deer in a nearby forest. It was twilight and as we sat quietly waiting it began to rain gently. After some time I mentioned that I had always had a longing to dance naked in the rain. 'Be my guest,' was the response. With sudden daring, I slipped out of my clothes, left the car and danced in the rain. It felt fantastic, daring, outrageous, and I loved every minute. I'll probably never have the opportunity again, but for those few minutes, being outrageous felt like one of the sanest things I'd ever done.

How powerfully we are controlled by convention: I recall the day I went shopping with my husband. Having chosen trousers and a jacket the salesman turned Alan's attention to the tie rack. He pulled out one or two and held them against my husband's chest. 'Oh he'll never wear anything like that,' I said. 'He always likes very sober, dark-coloured ties.' My husband looked at me for a moment, grinned, and then turned back to the salesman and said, 'Actually, my wife always buys my ties – that's the way she sees me.'

I had really imagined that that was the way he liked to be seen, but what I had actually been doing was placing upon him my conventional pictures of how I thought he ought to look. Tolerant as he was, he had quietly gone along with it.

After this, I noticed he sometimes bought clothes I

considered a bit outrageous and I didn't like them at all. I thought the colours too feminine or the style not quite 'him'. I only realize now that I was slightly embarrassed, fearing people might see him as appearing too 'way-out'. I hope I've learnt better!

Pam and I found courage together to be outrageous. We would paddle in the sea in January, our skirts pulled up past our knees, ignoring the stares of passers-by who thought we were completely mad.

Obviously I am not suggesting that you do anything that is going to cause pain to another, or upset people too much – but daring to be outrageous occasionally, like laughter, is a good tonic.

Daring to express your humour needs a belief in your right to do so. People will frown at your laughter, they will glare at you as if you have suddenly dropped your trousers, they will try to give the impression that only the very lowest of the low would behave in such a manner. They'll also probably die before you from stomach ulcers – they haven't learnt that laughter helps to keep you alive.

I hope parts of this book make you smile. I hope you have some fun in reading it and trying out some of the exercises. I promise you that if you do you'll remember them.

10

Dare to Face Your Fears

Daring to face your fear and then meeting it head on is the very best way of dealing with it. Hiding it does not make fear go away, no matter how much we try to convince ourselves.

There are areas in which we all have problems with this – fear exists in all of us. I am not talking about survival fear, but of the fear that restricts freedom and prevents you from being the person you want to be.

Fear can come in many forms. Below are listed some of the fears you may find are limiting your life. Write down any others of your own that come to mind – perhaps there are ones you have never before admitted to another soul. Don't stop to analyse your thoughts at this point, just let any old fear that pops into your head take form and add it to your list.

Fear of failure	Fear of rejection
Fear of ridicule	Fear of being misunderstood
Fear of people's reactions	Fear of what people will say
Fear of what people will think	Fear of not being liked

Fear of the unknown   Fear of change

Fear of commitment   Fear of being hurt

Do you recognize one or more of these in yourself?

We worry so much about our image. We even worry what people will think about us when we don't even know them and are never going to meet them again. Take away other people and most of our fears disappear.

This tells us that most of what we fear lies within our concept of how we believe others perceive us. Where we think we do not measure up to their standards, we see it as a reflection of our inadequacies. It's terribly sad to think that we are ruled by such fears. What difference will it make if some people don't like you, or disapprove of what you do? Compare it with what you will gain by daring to pursue your goals.

You may want to return to college, but you are much older than all the other students and imagine you will look silly. Perhaps you are thinking that they will resent you, or mock you. So what? If it's what you really want to do, are you going to let such thoughts stop you? The chances are that when you get there they will enjoy having an older person to confide in. They may enjoy showing you the ropes, and you will almost certainly earn their respect if you conduct yourself with enthusiasm and work hard.

Many fears originate from our early formative years. In order to deal with them, go back to Exercise Two and use that exercise to free yourself from those incidents you now see as being instrumental in causing you to feel any of the following: self-conscious, shy, embarrassed, unsure, afraid to say or do certain things, afraid of being disliked or rejected.

When we are young and vulnerable, anything that isolates us from the pack can have a devastating effect upon how we perceive ourselves or value ourselves. If we are different in some way, we think the fault must lie within us.

Imagine now, as an adult, how you feel about a new situation – this could be viewing a new school for your children, a prospective job, the Women's Institute, or a social function. You may feel slightly conspicuous, aware that people are looking at you, wondering about you. You haven't done anything wrong – you should be warmly welcomed – so why the uncomfortable feelings? Fear of the unknown, perhaps? It is, however, much more likely to be a re-stimulation of childhood feelings when, for some reason, you felt isolated from the rest.

I have known a number of people who feel they will not be liked because of the way they look. If this is your problem, remember that you are unique and that you only have to be yourself.

Once you talk about your fears they seem much easier to handle. Some years ago, my family became friendly with a lovely girl who very easily became embarrassed. Whenever she experienced these feelings, she always told us. We found this very endearing and always went out of our way to make her feel at home and comfortable. By expressing her feelings she opened the door that let us in to help her deal with them.

In a new job, if you're feeling very nervous, tell somebody. Ninety-nine times out of a hundred they will then help you to feel better, make allowances, and show you the ropes.

Wanting to parachute jump, learning to swim, joining a gym, driving a car will all be made easier if you voice your fears. If you pause long enough to put yourself in the other person's place, you'll know that they will make it easier for you just as you would for them if the roles were reversed.

Many people take on an aggressive attitude, not necessarily to intimidate others, but to hide their own fears and feelings of inadequacy.

In my work as a consultant I have met many very well-dressed, well-groomed, outwardly sophisticated women, who tell me they feel inferior, have no friends, and believe that no one likes them. The problem is that by presenting themselves as they do, they hide the real person, and other women feel they can't measure up to what they see as a very high standard.

Looking beneath the veneer can be very revealing. As my granny used to say, *Never judge a sausage by its skin*. The lesson to be learned here is not simply one about understanding other people, but one which needs to be applied to ourselves. What messages are we sending out to others in our endeavour to hide what we see as our inadequacies?

I am always telling people that our imaginations rule our world and that most fears are imagined, and this is true. We picture what might happen, we imagine the resulting rejection, ridicule, failure, and so on, and those imagined pictures prevent us ever daring to make changes, aim for our goals, or be different.

Never judge a sausage by its skin.

Let us take a look at what we mean by failure, for it is one of the most powerful deterrents to daring to be or to do.

You have an image of what you want to achieve: it is desirable and attractive. This can be a one-off thing, such as taking a flight in a hot-air balloon, or it may be a goal that will change your life, like applying for the post of manager in the store where you work. Having decided that it is something you *really* want to do, what is your next step? Possibly, for a little while, you allow yourself some positive daydreams – things are still feeling good. And then you go and spoil it all by asking yourself what will happen if it doesn't work out. You change the positive images into negative ones. Failure feels painful; you withdraw feeling disappointed, at the same time telling yourself that it would never have worked for you. *It all happened in your imagination*.

Now you begin to see what I mean by your imagination ruling your world. If you can so control your life with negative pictures, you can do the opposite. You can *make* things happen by positively visualizing success.

Take time to remember and picture your successes. You have many, believe me. There was a time when you couldn't walk, talk, read, ride a bike, take a phone message, travel alone, swim, drive a car, manage money – the list is really endless. Now you can do most of those things and a whole lot more.

I have used this way of thinking with my own grandchildren when they have been afraid to try something new. 'Remember when you couldn't ride a bicycle?' I say. 'Think how many times you lost your balance, fell off, got on again, and kept on trying until you could do it.' They pause and look at me. It was only a few months ago and now they are able to do almost any trick on a bike. They recall the feeling of achievement and smile. 'That's how it will feel when you have learned to do this new thing,' I assure them. And suddenly they want to do it, for

success is a good feeling. Nothing has happened externally, only now they are focused on the *positive* aspects of
what they want to achieve.

Finding out how to do something, trying different ways
of getting there, is not failure, only learned experiences.
Scientists do experiments thousands of times in order to
discover something new and how it works. If they stopped
the first time an experiment didn't work the way they had
hoped, we would still be without drugs and living without
electricity.

There is no need to be intimidated by the experts of this
world. An expert is simply someone who appears to know
more about certain things than you do. When you are sure
that they do and that they are not creating this illusion to
support their beliefs about themselves, ask their advice or
help. Mature, well-balanced people are willing to pass on
their knowledge – it is flattering to be asked.

To be honest with ourselves, and to open the door to
learning, we need to recognize that often, if we could do
something without being observed, then failure wouldn't
matter. This is a reminder of just how much we are allowing what other people think of us to restrict our life.

A lady I knew told me of a fear she had that something
terrible was going to happen to her. She thought this
overpowering feeling was a premonition of death. The
strange thing was that this paralysing feeling came at the
same time each night; about an hour later it would fade
away, only to return the following evening. Finally she
decided she could stand no more. That night she went to
her room, sat on a chair and spoke to her fearful self: 'Go
on then, kill me. Just get on with it. I can't live like this
anymore so you might as well finish me off.' She waited.
The appointed hour came and went. Nothing happened.
At last she gave up waiting and wondered what would
happen the following night. Her fear never returned.
Once she decided to confront her fear, it lost its power.

Fear is only in the mind. It can, of course, be transmitted to your body, but it all starts in your head. Your behaviour is totally ruled by the images you create. See yourself succeed, tell yourself that you can do so, and all that remains is to follow it through.

Fear of Commitment

I know a man who is so determined never to have children that at the age of 29 he went to see his doctor in the hopes that he would agree to a vasectomy. The sad thing is that this man is extremely fond of children but believes he may not be a good father. He is afraid to commit himself in case he fails. This belief, *without any foundation*, is preventing him from enjoying one of the most rewarding experiences life has to offer.

He is not alone. Many people fearing other people's high expectations of them, hold back. Others, believing that they will be put-upon, or pushed beyond their limits, also shy away from commitment.

When asked if we will do something, many of us condition our responses in ways that tell of our fears: *It depends what it is. I'm not sure if I can. I'd rather you didn't ask me to do anything right now*.

It really is refreshing when you need help to hear 'What can I do for you?' or 'How can I help?'

Daring to commit yourself all the way in something is a great motivator. We see this demonstrated in people who work for charities, who go out under fire to help those who are suffering or commit themselves totally to raising money for research; and in parents who may commit themselves to a life of caring for a physically or mentally disabled child. Total commitment elevates people to a higher level of living – in many cases it becomes a way of life that is completely selfless and at the same time wonderfully inspiring.

If you have ever longed to commit yourself to something and perhaps, in a way, felt disappointed in yourself that you have never achieved that goal, take a good look at why you have never allowed yourself to go ahead. Could it be fear? Fear of failure, of not being able to see it through, or perhaps of getting too involved?

I have spoken with people who have longed to foster a child but are scared they will grow too fond of it and could not bear the pain of having it taken from them. They are afraid to commit themselves because of the fear of this pain, and so deny themselves great joy and fulfilment.

Quite recently I was counselling a widow who had backed off from a second marriage in case the new man for whom she had grown to care for, might also die and leave her. She saw being alone as better then the happiness that was available – in case it didn't last!

Exercise Nine – Facing Up to Commitment

Fulfilment through commitment means that you have to face your fears and deal with them. This can be helped by using visualization.

1 Close your eyes and take three very deep breaths and relax. Think about what it is you would like to commit yourself to but have, until now, been afraid to do so. (To begin with, make this something that is not too challenging – you can progress to greater commitments when smaller ones have been achieved.)

2 Ask yourself what is it that is holding you back from this commitment. Recognize it for what it is. It may be something from the past, or the fear of not being able to live up to expectations, or the fear of pain, or of rejection. Picture yourself in that negative situation.

3 Now superimpose over that picture a wonderful positive picture of the future within your grasp. Play around with this picture of how life can be when you totally commit yourself to it – add colour, sound, anything that makes it come alive. Make it attractive. Make it desirable.

4 Repeat this from the beginning several times, allowing the old picture to become less and less distinct as the future one grows in intensity and reality.

5 Now tell yourself how you will achieve this and when you will start.

Note: So many people live in a 'if only' world and never turn it into reality. Now you have fixed a time make sure you follow it through. This is the commencement of your commitment.

When you are afraid to do such things as climb a ladder, fly in an aeroplane or shop alone, and the fear seems to have nothing to do with anyone else, it is usually linked to your survival system. Although there may, in reality, be no more danger in climbing a ladder than crossing the road, you feel threatened and an exaggerated reaction takes over. Often this then develops into a phobia. Such fears can result from a previous trauma or a learned behaviour pattern.

The fear *can* still be in worrying about other people's reactions – *what will people think of me if I get stuck half-way up the ladder?* Agoraphobia may not be fear of open spaces, but fear of what people will think of you if you panic, can't get to a toilet in time, or show yourself up in some other unacceptable way.

Whatever the fear, if it is not life-threatening but is

restricting you or spoiling the quality of your life, you can deal with it by using the following visualization exercise. This exercise includes a complete relaxation induction.

Exercise Ten – Undoing Responses to Past Traumas

1 Make yourself comfortable and relax. Look across the room and focus your eyes on something in front of you. Anything will do – a picture, a mark on the wall, a lamp. As you continue to focus on that spot, begin counting slowly backwards from 500 quietly to yourself. Continue counting until you feel your eyes getting tired and wanting to close. As soon as they feel ready to close, let them go. (Don't struggle to keep them open, they will naturally begin to feel tired or watery and start to blink.) Let everything happen naturally.

2 When your eyes have closed, stop counting and mentally check that each part of your body is completely relaxed. Feel your toes relax, your legs, your body. Allow a calm peaceful expression to pass across your face, let your mouth and lips relax. Imagine all the stress and tension from your head, neck and shoulders, flowing down your arms and out through the tips of your fingers. Be comfortably aware of the feelings and sensations in your body as you relax.

3 Identify your problem. Ask yourself: Does it have a secondary gain? Does it allow something to happen that is more important to me? If the answer is yes, you must deal with the secondary gain first – if you don't, it will only manifest itself in some other way. (Should you feel that you can't handle this yourself, consult a therapist.) If there is no secondary gain you can now undo your emotional responses to that past trauma.

4 Picture yourself going into an empty cinema. You can
   imagine someone with you if you feel better that way.
   You make your way between the seats until you are
   roughly in the centre and you then pull down a seat, sit on
   it, and look at the screen. On the screen you create a
   picture of yourself just before you experience those bad
   feelings. See this picture in black and white, a bit faded
   perhaps so that it is not too clear. If you can recall when it
   first happened, what caused your fear, then go back to
   that first occasion. If you have no memory of where it
   came from or how it started, use the pictures that come
   into your mind when you think of those bad feelings, or
   the phobia. What, exactly, do you imagine is going to
   happen? Even if in reality it has never happened, use the
   pictures of what you imagine *might* happen. These can be
   just as powerful in causing a phobia. You may picture the
   plane in which you fly crashing – it hasn't done so because
   fear may have prevented you from ever leaving the ground,
   but use those pictures, imagined or real.

5 With the 'just before' picture of yourself on the screen,
   imagine that you float up from your seat in the cinema
   into the projection room. From here you can look down
   and see yourself still sitting in the seat. You can also still
   see that picture of yourself on the screen. (Putting yourself in the projection room in this way is done to help
   you separate yourself from the experience you are about
   to watch.) You have the controls in your hand and can
   switch the pictures on or off as you choose. It is not
   necessary to imagine yourself going through that experience again, you need only to picture it from a distance.
   If you think it may still feel too real, visualize a glass
   panel or filter between you and the cinema screen. You
   now press the controls and turn it into a movie. Watch
   it right through to just beyond the end and then stop the
   picture.

6 Imagine that you press a switch and turn that picture into colour. You now jump *into* the picture and run it backwards. Everything happens in reverse. Everything happens backwards. Take just a few seconds to do this. (Help yourself along verbally if you find that helps.)

7 Open your eyes and take note of your surroundings. Pause for a few moments then close them again. Now picture yourself without the fear, feeling completely free to do that thing. Without your fear, what can you now do? Adjust this new positive picture of yourself until it looks and feels good. (If you still have any doubts repeat the whole process, speeding up the part where you are in the picture and running it backwards.)

8 Count slowly backward from five to one, open your eyes and return to full conscious awareness and feel really pleased with your new-found confidence.

Note. This visual exercise can be done by imagining yourself watching the TV screen in your own home with exactly the same results. However, if it is a really powerful fear, using the cinema screen and removing yourself to the projection room will give you a sense of distance and control.

This exercise is very effective and can be used in many different situations, and I have never known it to fail when it is done properly.

Daring to be Different

Have you ever wished you could step off the treadmill of convention? Have you longed to behave in a way that seems to violate the standards you were taught as a child? Have you ever wanted to give up your steady job and do something so completely different that all your family and friends might be shocked? Some people do.

Daring to do something seen as different, means stepping away from the security of 'the herd'. You will recall that earlier I wrote of how, as children, it was so important for us to be and do like everyone else; it makes us feel safe. Now, as an adult, you should be able to stand alone, to make your own way, to dare to be individual – to be different. This ought not to be through a desire to draw attention to yourself, or to make a statement due to an underlying insecurity; it should be because you genuinely wish to do or be something that is not possible when you constantly conform to a certain image.

In order to dare to be different you have to build your ego, your sense of feeling okay about being yourself. You need to set yourself free from being controlled by what other people think.

This is not pure self-indulgence – it is fulfilling a need, developing your true self. Such an experience can be delightfully refreshing; it may change your life, it could be the biggest contribution you make to the world. It can be a tiny thing that almost goes unnoticed, except for the way you feel about it.

Many people I get to know tell me, 'This isn't me at all, I'm not really like this inside.' They don't want to go on acting a part, but they don't know how to stop.

As long as we behave in a way that does not harm others, we have the right to pursue our own path. Parents who throw up their hands in horror and talk about being let down, shown up, or disappointed by their children, have lost sight of what parenthood is all about. Of course we want the best for our children, but when they have reached an age where they take responsibility for their own lives, we have to stop imposing our own ideas.

Maybe your child doesn't want a steady job, or to follow in dad's footsteps at the cricket club, or get married and start a family. Some children are going to roam the world, get involved in the arts, reject sport completely, be non-competitive. Others will explore and pursue things you never dreamed of doing.

I do believe that we all need to be responsible for ourselves. Expecting to be supported by a state welfare system does no one any good. To develop a sense of self-worth we need to make our own way and also to make our own contribution. Having said that, we still cannot impose these beliefs on another.

For you, being different may mean joining a theatrical group, sleeping out on the beach, working with your hands instead of your brain, speaking out instead of always blending with the crowd. It is your life, live it to the utmost, give it everything you've got.

Pause here, and for a few minutes consider the following.

- In what way do you want to be different?

- Is there anything to really prevent you?

- How will you set about it?

Remember, positive visualization is extremely powerful. Picturing things in your mind and seeing the outcome you desire, will give you the courage and confidence to carry through and achieve your objectives.

Making Decisions

There are few things more infuriating than people who will not make decisions. There are also times when all of us hesitate and try to avoid doing so.

Making decisions can be exhilarating, it can also fill us with fear and trembling. *What if I get it wrong, say the wrong thing, create a disastrous situation?* You will, no doubt, have had these or similar thoughts hover in your brain from time to time. The truth is, that if you fail to make a decision, you have actually made one – you have decided to do nothing about the situation.

Leaving the decision making to someone else puts the responsibility on their shoulders. Are you afraid of taking the blame should things go wrong? Of looking foolish? Of failing in some way?

When you look at the people in this world who make things happen, the leaders in business, people in authority, the one thing they have in common is the ability to make decisions.

If you have to constantly be asking for approval from a higher authority before doing something, you will never progress – you will never build a sense of self-worth either.

Begin to notice your decision ability and build on what you find. Do you make positive decisions in a restaurant when you read the menu? Or do you ask someone else to choose? When you go out for the evening, do you decide where to go, or do you always leave it to the other person? And who decides what colour to emulsion the walls of your home, or what to plant in the garden?

Every time you allow someone else to decide for you, your confidence is eroded. It is easier to start making decisions at a social and domestic level. If you have been having problems in these or other similar areas of your life, make a decision *now* to start by saying where you would like to go and what you would like to eat.

It may be that you have problems at work and feel the need to have someone endorse your decisions before putting them into practice. If you are up to the job – and presumably the management think so or they wouldn't be paying your salary – start making your own decisions. Of course you will make wrong ones occasionally, but that's how we all learn.

Changing jobs, investing money, buying or moving house, getting married or starting a family, are big decisions which most of us will have to make at some time in our lives, so it is as well to get into practice before those really big ones come along.

To make decisions, you must first deal with the fear. When you find yourself hesitating and not knowing what to do or say, ask yourself what is it exactly that you are afraid of? You will be surprised to discover how often your fear is the result of another childhood experience. A very strict parent or exacting teacher can create such fear in a child that he is afraid to say or do almost anything.

However, you are no longer that vulnerable child and decision-making actually helps put you in control. Certainly consider the options first; then, having taken a good look at them, make your decision. With practice, it becomes easier and easier, until decision-making takes its rightful place amongst the many other things you now do naturally as a responsible adult.

11

Changing Your Image

You wish you looked different. You want people to see you differently. One way or another you are not pleased with the way you present yourself to the world.

Thanks to modern science, if we really want to change our appearance – and if doing so would help us to a healthier, happier way of living – it is possible.

I know of a young girl who is having surgery on her nose because it makes her feel so conspicuous and self-conscious that she won't leave the house. It is sad to think that one's appearance should become such a handicap, but for her this operation seems the only way. However, if she had a better self-image and was able to have fun and made friends, she might, quite possibly, have not been in the least bit concerned about her appearance.

Many times we think it is our appearance that stops people liking us when we are actually using this as an excuse. Well-balanced people like us for what we are, not the way we look. Should your appearance be something you want to improve and you *can* do something about it, now is the time to get started.

If you have put off going to a gym because you think the people there will all be fitter and slimmer and look better than you, you are wrong. Most of them will have started off with, and probably still have, similar problems to your own. What is more, people like you more if they do not feel threatened by you.

Exercise can be done in solitude. Walking is an excellent exercise. Using a cycling- or rowing-machine is another way of building muscles and getting fit.

There are a thousand or more diets that claim to help you lose weight. Eating less, and sensibly, will get the same results if combined with exercise.

So what is stopping you from looking slim and fit? Could it be fear? Many forms of change offer a threat: *How will I cope? What will people think? What if I can't stick at it?* If you don't like your changed image you can always revert to the old one. However, I wouldn't mind betting that you will prefer your new image.

The country now has hundreds of beauty clinics where staff are trained to help people just like you. So if you want to change, go along and seek their advice. The advice usually comes free – they make their money out of selling you the treatments and the products.

Changing your image, your hairstyle, your dress, may give your morale a tremendous boost, but unless you also view yourself positively it won't work permanently.

Know why you want to change your image and make sure the reasons make sense. If we don't like the way we are and feel unacceptable to others, we all too readily blame our appearance for all our problems. This is especially so when we are struggling through the agonies of the teenage years and falling in love.

It is worth asking yourself why it is that a girl who never wears make-up, bothers little with her clothes or hair, and is actually quite plain, should be so popular with the boys. Is it perhaps because she is simply good fun to be with, or doesn't make a relationship heavy-going? Is she gentle or compassionate, or just a good listener?

A lad I knew some years ago had a mohican hair-cut. At the time it was almost unheard of – certainly not seen in our small town. He also had his ears pierced and wore several rings in them. One day, when we were talking, I asked him why he chose the hair-cut. 'People look at it and don't see me,' he replied. The sad thing was that they then judged him as a yob or trouble-maker when in fact he was a self-conscious, quiet boy with many good qualities.

As with all things, you need to look at the intention behind the act. Perhaps it isn't your image that needs to change but the way you see yourself. If you are confident, you don't need to make statements with your appearance.

Exercise Eleven – Changing Your Image

1 Close your eyes and relax. Imagine standing in front of a mirror. See your reflection exactly as you are. Start at the top of your head and note each detail. Appreciate the good things – texture of skin, colour of eyes, shape of face or forehead, strength in arms, etcetera.

2 Now note the thing or things you want to change. Maybe you wish to be slimmer, or to change the colour of your hair – they might be possible changes. You make your decision.

3 Lean forward and press a button on the side of the mirror. This allows it to rotate, presenting to you the other side. Here you see yourself with the changes already made. Take a good look. Do you like the changes?

4 When they feel right – and you can change whatever you want, provided they are possible changes – step into

the mirror and experience how it feels. Take your time to do this thoroughly.

5 If you like the changes, you are ready to go ahead and put them into practice.

Note: If the changes did not feel right for you, leave it a few days and do this exercise again.

Daring to do it Anyway

It would be reassuring to have a guarantee with everything before we tried it, but we wouldn't learn much from such experiences.

We learn much more from our mistakes than from getting things right first time. Learning to drive a car is a very good example of this. Where you took a bend too fast and nearly lost control you learnt in one lesson how to take bends in the future. If you *happened* to have taken the bend at the right speed, slowing a little as you approached it and then gently accelerating around it, you wouldn't have known how you did this. It wasn't until you got it wrong that you learnt exactly how *not* to take a bend and also how to do it properly.

Can you imagine if every time you bought an item of clothing you absolutely *knew* it would fit and that it would suit you? There would be no anticipation, no sense of expectancy – you would never learn about style or the harmony of colour. It would all just 'be'.

One of the things I disliked most when I was in engineering was having to go out and get orders. I felt as if I was selling myself. If the manager, or boss, or buyer didn't like me, he was never going to even let me start talking about our plant or what we could produce.

When I became a writer I thought things would be

completely different. I would be able to concentrate on being creative and let someone else do the marketing. I now know better! Writing is the easy bit; it is the selling that is so hard. Before people bought my books *I* had to be sold to them as a 'personality' or 'expert'. Until I faced this problem and dealt with it, it was going to keep on presenting itself.

So why did I dislike it? The answer was that I didn't know how I was going to be received. Once when I knew, without any doubt, that the person I was meeting liked my work and wanted to buy it, I could actually enjoy the interview.

However, there are no guarantees in living. You have to dare to anyway.

By all means consider the objective and the consequences of your actions, and then, so long as they are not life-threatening, take a chance. If you don't, you will never know what you may have missed or what you are capable of doing.

Suppose it goes wrong? says the doubter. *But suppose it goes right?* says the optimist.

Suppose they don't like me? says the man who fears. *But suppose they think I'm fantastic?* says the man who dares.

Suppose I lose everything? says the woman who dearly wants to develop a new idea but is afraid. *But suppose it is a success and helps thousands of people?* says the woman who will risk anything rather than live with a sense of something left untried.

Did you ever have a great longing to do something? And did you allow yourself to be talked out of it? Perhaps you were headstrong in those days, you may have been ambitious, you may have had a dream. How do you feel about it now? You may find comfort by assuring yourself that it was wiser or safer not to have done it, or it wouldn't have worked anyway, but underneath there is still that tiny pulsating thought *If only I had had the courage to do it anyway.*

In some ways it is easier when you are young to follow your heart's desire. People make allowances. You have health, energy, and enthusiasm on your side. At twenty, taking two years off from your career to wander the world is usually accepted with a tolerant smile – you would be hard put to do so with a mortgage and three children.

It is never too late to take a thought and turn it into a deed. It may need a 'what-the-hell' attitude, but I bet you will feel as if you've suddenly been given a million dollars after you have achieved it. Even achieving isn't essential, it's having had a go that makes you feel so good. This is why we see the most unexpected people attempting the marathon run. They are not all going to come in with the first ten, or even the first hundred – some will never complete the course – but can you imagine what it feels like to have made the attempt?

You want to do something that sounds quite crazy for a man or woman of 65. They tell you you'll look a fool, that it's just not you. Some will laugh and smirk and say 'I told you so', but deep down inside there will be a wistful longing, a wish that they had the courage to do what you have done. Whatever words they use, underneath you will have gained a respect that was never there before. 'He did a parachute jump – at his age! I ask you, isn't he a fool?' Do you hear the admiration behind the question?

Okay! You may be laughed at, ridiculed, scorned, but you did it! You dared to anyway. There's a deep feeling of satisfaction, of pride – and no one can take that away from you.

12

Dare to be Adventurous

This means different things to different people. It can mean sailing round the world, taking a flight in an aeroplane for the first time, learning to swim, choosing to live abroad. Being adventurous to you may mean applying for promotion or a new job, or something as simple as asking a neighbour to go for a walk with you. To a young man, asking someone for a date may seem more adventurous than crossing the Arctic on skis.

It starts with a thought, grows into a longing, and from here you allow it to manifest itself. This can happen after years of deliberation or it can be almost instantaneous. Evidence shows that people who are impulsive do tend to be more adventurous than those who spend much thought looking at a project from all angles before committing themselves. Sometimes, years of training are necessary before you can take the plunge. For example, mountain climbers have to reach peak fitness before they dare attack the summits.

You may want to start with some quite small thing, like taking a holiday alone. However big or small the adventurous thought in your mind may be, you have first to rid yourself of the doubts and fears (or both).

Ask yourself the right questions to get the right answers. Why do I want to do this? How will it benefit me (or my family, job or friends)? What is really holding me back? Are the things holding me back more important than my need to do this thing?

As I have explained in my book *Are You In Control?*, we motivate ourselves by enhancing the positive-outcome pictures in our minds. If we picture all the things that could go wrong when we go out, we would never step outside our own door.

If you want to date a girl and you imagine her turning you down, you will never ask. If you begin to think, *Well, she may say yes* (and why shouldn't she?), then you open the door of possibility. You begin to picture yourself with her. You make it look good, feel good – and you go ahead and ask her.

What to say on a new date is one of the greatest deterrents for most young people wanting to make new friends. It really doesn't matter what you talk about – if you don't believe me, listen in to a few conversations in a pub or on a bus. Talking about something that really interests you will make you come alive, and you will make it interesting to your friend. Obviously, talking about sports cars all night may possibly bore the girlfriend, so remember also to find out what interests her, and get her talking about that too. If neither of you has any interests that awaken you sufficiently to be able to talk for at least ten minutes on the subject, then *get interested*. You probably are boring and do need to open up your world. Holidays, films, books, music, school or college life are all safe subjects you can open up on with someone new. Don't be scared to share your ideas, they are what make you unique.

It is also worth noting that most of us feel intimidated by a brilliantly clever person. Being 'brainy' isn't a necessary requirement for a good relationship. Being kind and understanding is.

Have you ever done anything on impulse? It can be a fantastic feeling. When I was a teenager I accidentally boarded the wrong train and found myself on a non-stop excursion to London to a pantomime on ice. When this was discovered they offered to put me on the next train back – or I could go on to the show with the rest of the passengers. On impulse I said I would like to go. I was given *free*, one of the best seats in the theatre, a box of chocolates, and a free meal on the train coming home. I enjoyed myself tremendously – not only was the whole experience free, but I saw a most spectacular show that I would perhaps never have seen otherwise.

Being adventurous may mean proceeding with caution. It doesn't have to be a headlong plunge into the unknown.

Exercise Twelve – Daring to be Adventurous

1 Close your eyes, breathe deeply and relax. Think of an adventure that you would like to tackle, or indulge in. How would you set about it?

2 Imagine how it would feel. A bit scary, perhaps? Turn that scary feeling into excitement. The physical responses are the same – the speeding up of your heartbeats, tension in your muscles, dry mouth, shivers running down your spine. However you feel when you are scared, imagine now those same feelings being used to experience excitement.

3 How would you feel after your adventure? Perhaps you can imagine coming back home and telling people about it. What would you say? You most certainly will feel pleased with yourself that you used your courage so positively.

4 Now ask yourself, *Is there anything to stop me from doing this thing?* If there isn't, go ahead and enjoy the experience. If there is, see how you could overcome those obstacles.

13

Dare to Realize Your Dreams

Dreams remain dreams until we do something about them. Those thoughts that you never really take seriously never get anywhere. Conviction and real desire are missing.

So maybe you won't ever win the lottery, but if you want a lot of money – if that is what you *really* want – you can have it. Once you have firmly embedded your dream in belief, you can set about making it become a reality.

I have a friend who started life with £12 in his pocket and became a multi-millionaire. He bought an old van and took on jobs that no one else wanted. From this he saw further possibilities and actively pursued them. He bought old properties and did them up. He worked seven days a week. He thought constantly about how to use people's natural potential to produce money honestly. His goal was *not* to be rich – money, for him, was simply a measure of his success. His dream was to be a successful man.

Perhaps you have a dream to be recognized for your artistic talents but think you are not good enough. You are. If you learn to use the right side of your brain – the unconscious mind where creativity is born – you can produce wonderful original work. This doesn't mean you can bypass all the groundwork, the hours of training and study that must go into anything that is worthy of true art – but you can make it.

I personally know of no one who has become successful or fulfilled their dreams without a lot of self-sacrifice or hard work.

To realize your dream, look beneath the surface. Ask yourself what exactly it is that you want. It may be that you can achieve this in some other way.

For example, wanting to achieve something may be an unconscious need to be publicly recognized. You may not be able to do this by producing a new rose or writing a book, but you could do it by raising more money for charity than anyone else has yet done.

In an electrical supply shop recently, I asked the young man who served me whether he had any dreams for his future. Immediately he replied that he wanted to become manager as fast as he could and to own a nice car. His response told me at once that his dreams had become goals and he saw them as something he fully intended to achieve.

To make your dreams come true, see them as a reality. If they are totally impossible, change them around a bit so that the underlying need can still be met.

For many thousands of people, being able to retire early is a dream. They long to have the time to pursue their hobbies and interests, to travel while they can still get around, to enjoy the garden, to be free of the pressures and changing demands of a job. However, they still have to pay the mortgage, make sure there is enough in the pension fund to see them through years of retirement, and wait until the children have left home.

Let us take a look at how this dream could become a reality. Usually the problem is financial. So what about a part-time job? I know a young man of only 36 who has retired. He now works at his hobby in the morning, which brings in some income, and in the afternoon helps out in

There are few things more rewarding than making your dreams come true

a nursery. He doesn't have so much cash to spend but he is much happier than when he was working in a very demanding job.

Some partners change roles – the woman goes out to work while the man runs the home. Others use a facility set up by the insurance companies that releases some (or all) of the cash from their house, or guarantees an income for life set against the property. If you consider this route may be the right one for you, do take professional financial advice.

If you are in rented accommodation and your income is low, you may be eligible for assistance. In some cases your total rent will be paid by the authorities. If you have worked hard all your life, paid tax and made regular National Insurance contributions, you don't need to feel badly about being helped in this way.

You may think it impossible to get another job if you retire at 50 or 55, but so long as you are flexible there is still plenty of work around. I frequently see jobs offered on notice boards in shop windows, the local papers and in magazines.

A lady I know works one month on and one month off as a companion to an elderly widow. On her months off she spends her time writing and enjoying her home and garden. For her this works and she is very happy.

Being made redundant can be a very traumatic experience – your world may suddenly seem as if it is disintegrating and you may feel rejected and worthless. This is very sad because in fact nothing has changed – you are still exactly the same person you were before, whatever the reason given for dispensing with your services. Only now you are seeing yourself differently; because you have lost your job you feel something very bad has happened to you. It has, if you believe this to be so. However, if you learn to look for the good in every situation, you will see opportunities open up before you. If you allow it, your life can take on a new meaning in a completely different direction. You have been given the chance to have a try at something else. There may never be a better time to pursue your dreams and turn them into a reality. Redundancy is rather like retirement, you have to find a new purpose and direction in your life.

Alex had spent all his life working in an industry he loathed. At 58 he was offered early retirement. He knew he did not have enough pension to enable him and his wife to live comfortably, but he took the risk anyway; he was so fed up with his job. Almost immediately he was asked by a solicitor if he would like to work for the practice dealing with the effects of people who died. This often meant visiting bereaved elderly people, and Alex's natural compassion and caring, were soon put to good use. He was so delighted with how well he worked in this environment that ten years later he was still putting in an eight-hour day.

There are few things more rewarding than making your dreams come true. Unless they are a physical impossibility, there is usually some way of turning them into reality. Believing in your dream puts the positive energy in motion that helps things to come about.

14

Daring to be Creative

One of the greatest deterrents to being creative is the thought that other people will frown upon what we do. I once saw an exhibition made up entirely of old used cans. I thought it looked awful, but my admiration for the people who had put in so much thought and effort made the whole experience worthwhile.

Not everyone is going to applaud your efforts, but through them you may begin to grow in a way that can change your life for the better.

A very good example is the work of the Impressionists. Some of the earlier work of these artists was ridiculed, but it did lead to the wonderful paintings of people like Manet and Pissarro. Van Gogh, who was thought to be completely mad by conventional standards, produced paintings that have since sold for more than any other form of art.

'I could never do . . .' prevents you from ever opening your mind to your abilities and talents. *Don't even think it!*

Being creative means you are going to start being original too. When you begin to create, to think in a way that is entirely new, it puts you on a 'high'. You feel elevated, elated. This very positive form of energy seems to wipe away tiredness and depression; it certainly knocks any negative thoughts right off the scene.

Many people think that if they can't draw or paint they have no artistic ability. This often goes back to art lessons at school that were boring or disastrous. Don't let that put you off. Everyone has the ability to be creative. The way you arrange the furniture in your house, place a vase of flowers, choose the covers for your bed, are all demonstrations of your own creative and artistic ability.

Planting a garden is another example. The trouble is that most people underestimate this kind of creativity and believe they are totally unable to be creative, or think of anything original.

A gardening programme on television this very evening was advising us to look at how others design their gardens, but to feel free to interpret it in our own way. The garden has only to satisfy the artist in you.

Being creative is a very individual thing. If you like words, try writing poetry – it doesn't even have to rhyme. Just write your feelings about something that catches your imagination or inspires you. You can progress to doing it according to the rules later if you really want to. Start writing and you'll find that it gets better and better. No one has to read it or listen to it unless you decide you wish to share your thoughts and feelings in this way.

One of the cheapest creative hobbies is sketching: all you need is a pencil and a piece of paper. Auguste Rodin used to sit under the kitchen table and draw on old newspapers with a crayon when he was a child – and he became one of the world's most famous sculptors.

The biggest problem to overcome when drawing or sketching is to draw what you see and not what you think you see. The conscious, logical half of the brain needs to take a back seat when you have a pencil in your hand. A chair may have four legs of equal length but that's not the way they look when you draw them. Turning a picture upside down and copying it is a good way of learning to draw what you see. You can hardly stand on your head to do it and so are forced to draw it as it is. You'll be surprised at the results.

If you want to paint, take a piece of paper, dip your brush in a colour and let it run down the paper a bit. Then take another colour and do the same. After doing this several times look at what you have produced and note what you see in it – there may be vague shapes of houses, people, or animals. As you do this your creativity begins to take over. Now deliberately add a brush of colour to make something happen . . . and you're on your way. When we look at clouds or hills we often turn them into recognizable shapes inside our minds. That is your creative part at work.

Einstein is said to have discovered the theory of relativity by passing his half-formed thoughts over to his unconscious mind as he drifted into sleep. He awoke with the answer but then had to work backwards from this to develop his theorem. He recognized that creativity comes from the right-brain and not the verbal and logical left-brain.

Being inventive is another wonderful way of using your creative ability. You see a problem and look for ways to solve it. Your mind approaches this from many angles and then, if you have learned the trick, you stop consciously thinking about it and allow it to brew at an unconscious level. Suddenly the answer arrives, returning to the conscious left-brain where you proceed to design or manufacture the part.

Music and writing are two very rewarding ways of using your creative ability. Most composers and writers when asked how they created something will pause, go inward for the answer, and often return with, 'It was just there in my head.' Creativity is a gift. When you allow it to surface, your natural talent will manifest itself with very little conscious effort.

Carrying this through is where the real effort comes in. You may have the idea for a song, but writing it down and arranging it in the best possible way has still to be worked through.

Handcrafts, wood carving, glass engraving and welding can all be used to let your creative self find expression. It is fun, wonderfully therapeutic, and you have nothing to lose. I can promise you that you will never feel more alive, more complete, than when you are being creative.

To release your own creativity, do the following exercise. Read through it several times than place the book aside and give it a try.

Exercise Thirteen – Releasing Your Creativity

1 Make yourself comfortable, relax, and close your eyes. Breathe deeply. Notice the feelings in your body as you let go and relax.

2 Imagine that you are walking down a leafy country lane. You are wearing comfortable clothes and shoes. It is summertime and there is a faint perfume in the air from wild flowers. Insects are gently humming, and in the distance you hear the sounds of birds or a tractor at work.

3 Presently you find yourself walking alongside an old stone wall. There is a door in the wall and a latch that enables you to open it from the outside. This door opens the way to your creativity.

4 Press the latch, open the door, and walk inside.

5 You begin to explore this place. It may be a garden, a woodland, a playground, a house – whatever comes to mind that feels right for you. You may feel you want to

change things or create a new patch in the garden. Give your mind freedom, let it do what it chooses without criticizing or putting obstacles in the way.

6 Presently you find a seat where you can sit down and rest. As you relax, thoughts begin to drift into your head. You let these thoughts come and go as they please, knowing that one will stay with you and, because of its importance, you will carry it back with you to your everyday life. This is the beginning of something entirely new for you – just let it come.

7 When you are ready, count slowly backwards from five to one and open your eyes.

Note: You may not immediately know what this new thought is or where you will apply it. Don't worry. It will have taken root and soon, if you choose, you will find a way of using it.

You can go back to this exercise any time you want to expand your creativity. Some things will appear symbolically, others will instantly be clear.

When I am driving the car, or drifting off to sleep, or peeling vegetables at the kitchen sink, thoughts like this will come. I find I need to write down the ones that I am going to use in my creative writing or I lose them. Some just pop up as I am working at the computer exactly when they are needed.

When I am lecturing, an idea or thought that is entirely new often presents itself to me and I am able to share it with my class. Never worry about being at a loss for words or ideas – once you start communicating with the unconscious creative part of your mind, you can trust it to produce the things you need. The problem becomes not,

Where will they come from? but rather, *How can I cope with so many?* Then, of course, you can become selective.

15

Dare to be Still

We do not help others by making decisions for them or by allowing others to do so for us. Within each of us is the inner wisdom to find our own answers. By being quiet sometimes and turning inwards we can tap that source.

Everything you have ever seen, heard, done or experienced, is recorded in the brain. We are not always conscious of this but it is true. Learning to trust yourself and to listen to your inner voice can be more beneficial than reading a hundred books or listening to a thousand voices.

We are all intuitive, although it is not always a sense that is acknowledged. The more you use your intuition, the more it will make itself known to you. You may well have had a feeling when driving, that around the next bend in the road there will be an obstacle. You slow the car, approach with caution, and perceive a large vehicle bearing down on you – that is your intuition at work. You feel intuitively when you can trust someone. You have a feeling when a house is just right for you.

Using your intuition allows it to become more active. Listening to it can be so inspiring that you will wonder how you ever came to neglect it for so long. The trouble is that we are afraid of silences. We feel we ought to be doing *something* always, or we feel guilty. Being comfortable with oneself is not easy. Unwanted thoughts creep in to disturb any chance of tranquillity.

In the Eastern world people are taught differently-they have learned the value of listening to their inner voice. A certain 'sense' tells them when to plant crops, when to move their cattle on, when to prepare for death. We may call the superstitions of uneducated people primitive nonsense, but the truth is that it works.

When you decide to get to know your inner self, don't feel ashamed or guilty. This is not self-indulgence but learning how to use another sense that is a part of you. To use your intuition you have to allow the unconscious mind to work for you. You have to trust in its ability to provide you with all that you need to know. Be still, quiet your mind, and listen to your inner voice.

It is true that by taking the initiative we can make things happen – but sometimes we simply need to allow them to come about. If you take a look at the prospectus of your local evening classes, you will almost certainly see that there is a course on meditation or self-awareness. Slowly, we are recognizing the need to be still.

Sitting on a deck chair on the beach or lazing in front of the TV does not allow you to contact your inner self. Being still, means *still* in every sense of the word. At first you may find this difficult. Taking something and contemplating it, getting so involved in it that you temporarily lose awareness of your surroundings, is a good place to begin. You may choose something as simple as a petal from a flower, a word, a piece of wood – try to *become* it. How does it feel to be a petal falling from a flower, to land on a grass verge, to have a velvet skin, to feel drops of dew roll across you, to be lifted by a breeze and glide on the air?

Doing this helps to halt the clamouring voices – you stop

observing yourself from the outside and experience yourself from the inside. Don't try to make anything happen, just allow yourself to be.

Stillness can be very frightening. To be abandoned on a deserted island sounds terrifying to most of us. Having an animal or pet of some kind to talk to is better than total silence. There are some who cannot cope for a single day without the sounds of other people. Do you need to have a radio on to fill the silence? Do you go in search of company after a few hours of being alone? Do you feel that something is wrong if you speak to no one all day?

Living 24 hours without any outside contact of any kind can be very revealing. Learning to enjoy your own company and to feel at peace with yourself means that you do not constantly clamour for other people in order to see your own reflection.

When you are quiet and still you will discover the world around you is teeming with life and that nature makes its

Having a pet to talk to is better than total silence.

own music. Stand perfectly still in the countryside for ten minutes and you will see and hear things you never noticed were there before.

There are many ways to communicate with the world around you. Being still and listening with your inner mind helps you to focus in a new way on what you are. You are part of life and all it contains and is – you are not separate from it. Everything within and without is part of you and you are part of the oneness of the universe. There are no dividing lines. Separation only exists in the mind.

Daring to be still gives you a new confidence, it sets you free from the limitations of conscious thought and adds a new dimension to your life.

16

Dare to Stay Young

When I was a teenager I was fortunate enough to get to know a neighbour who helped change my life. He most certainly passed on to me many of his philosophies about life. This he did, not with words, but by example.

It all began when I decided I would like to learn to play the violin. Frank Honor agreed to teach me. His house was an Aladdin's cave: books were piled high on every seat and in order to sit down they had to be dumped on the floor. Treasures he had discovered on his exploration of the surrounding countryside were scattered everywhere – these might be anything from an old bone to a piece of rock. On the kitchen table a fresh loaf of bread, a pat of butter and a jar of home-made jam always stood in readiness in case someone felt hungry.

I don't think he ever noticed what he ate. His mind was far too busy enjoying life. On dustbin days he would wander down the street exploring the contents, salvaging things other people had discarded as useless. From these he built wonderful working models of steam engines. He also made contour maps that were exact in every detail.

Some days we would cycle to the coast searching for

fossils. Other times we would sit silent, side by side, painting the beautiful scenery.

Because he loved music, on Sundays he visited one of the local churches – not because he was a religious man, but because it had the best organ in town.

Frank didn't know how to grow old – there wasn't time. He was so interested in everything and listened with as much care to my words as he would have to the Queen of England.

Some years after I had married and left the district, I returned to Taunton and met Frank in the street. He had suffered a stroke that had affected his speech and he now needed a stick to support him when he walked.

His delight at seeing me was heart-warming. 'You must come back and see what I've been doing,' he said, turning in the direction of his home. Curious, I followed.

Unable to get far, and never having learned to drive, he had converted his little back garden into a haven for birds. They must have loved it there for the garden was filled with the sound of their song. He pointed to the bench he had erected. 'I sit here for hours studying them,' he told me. 'Do you know that . . .' And he was off, his mind still as alive as it had ever been. He reminded me of a very enthusiastic schoolboy. He had never grown old.

It is so easy to give up, to admit to age as a restrictor, when what we should be doing is to look at all the other doors it opens. There is always something new and wonderful to discover – often things we have previously completely overlooked.

Science now tells us that if we keep using our minds and exercising our bodies there is no need to suffer the limitations and many of the indignities of growing old.

Making love is a wonderful way of keeping young. It doesn't have to be accomplished in the way you once did. Love-making and a sense of fulfilment can be experienced without full intercourse taking place. When a couple grow old together they make allowances for the changes that take place physically and can still find each other delightfully attractive and desirable.

When you hear older people saying that they feel young at heart, they mean it. Also, you find that inside your head you are really very little different from the way you felt at 20. What you do gain is wisdom and patience – everything doesn't have to happen *now*, which is strange when you realize how little time you have left. It was when you had so much time that you felt you had to have things instantly, or make them happen immediately.

An elderly friend of mine found one very positive thing about growing older. 'You can be as eccentric as you like,' she told me. 'If you don't want to go somewhere or do something you just say so. They put it down to your being old and a bit eccentric or awkward; it gives you a wonderful sense of freedom.' She really cashed in on this and had a wonderful time before she died doing all the crazy things she had never dared to do while she was young. Worrying about what other people thought of her didn't matter anymore.

I once heard Jung being interviewed. He was asked his advice about growing old and staying as mentally alert and productive as he was. 'Live life as if you expect to reach 200,' he replied.

Our society looks at putting us out to graze after about 50. This need not be so. Change direction, learn a new skill, develop a new talent, but *don't* let them put you in the garbage can.

They say, *You are as old as you feel*. I believe it would be more accurate to say, *You are as old as you think*.

All this does not mean that you have to fly around at the pace of a teenager, or wear skirts half-way up your thighs. Certainly do so if that's what you want, but what I am talking about is something that goes much deeper – an attitude for life.

If you have allowed old age and stagnation to set in, all is not lost. Start by doing something new. There are plenty of adult education classes, clubs and activity centres for you to choose from. You could do anything from pottery to learning Greek. It will also give you the opportunity to mix with younger people. Clubs for the elderly can be comforting but are often too limiting. Get yourself out at least twice a week where you exercise with other people. This is a great motivator and is also much easier than disciplining yourself to exercise alone. There are many keep-fit and swimming sessions for the over 50s. They are cheaper too!

17

Dare to Succeed

When I was working as a sports psychologist I met with a number of top international players who had one common problem: pressure from being at the top made them want to fail. It wasn't always obvious at first, but when they recognized this they admitted that when they were at the top there was nowhere else to go and people's expectations became unbearable. Each time they went out to perform, whether it was golf, snooker, cricket or swimming, there was that nagging thought, *Will I be able to do it this time?*

To succeed we have to totally believe that a thing is possible. Some people may dream about swimming for their country, owning a fashion house, running a newspaper, but most start much further down the ladder. They set their sights on a possible goal and then, as they achieve it, they keep shifting it up towards the top. It is most unlikely that any prime minister has ever planned to be in that position before entering politics.

This doesn't mean you cannot have a goal to be the best, or reach the top in your career, but it is much easier if you set goals that can be achieved along the way, thus giving you encouragement to go on to the next.

To be successful in any area of your life you must have belief in yourself and a sense of purpose. Success isn't accidental, it is intentional, whether you consider it at a conscious or unconscious level.

Inside most us is the desire for recognition. We thrive on praise from the moment we begin to understand what smiles and nods of approval mean. There is also success that goes unnoticed because it is not what the majority see as outstanding achievement. In no way let this negate what you have set out to do or what you have achieved.

Should your one aim in life be to make a success of your marriage and you do just that, it is for you as great an achievement as climbing the Eiger is for someone else. Staying home and successfully bringing up a family is one of the most worthwhile achievements one can accomplish but, sadly, due to outside pressures and public opinion, mothers who stay at home often feel they have achieved nothing.

We thrive on praise . . .

What will enable you to reach your goal and be successful is your sense of purpose. If you watch a golf player about to hit the ball, at that moment he has only one objective in life – to make the ball go exactly where he wants it to go. You have to be like that golfer. Your sense of purpose must not waiver. There will be times when you feel disheartened, when almost everything appears to be going against you, but you must not give up. Keep determined, no matter what, to win through and get there.

Every human being is born with talents. To be successful we need only to recognize these and then build our lives or career around them. Using a talent is not difficult, it comes as naturally as breathing. It is given to you at birth – all you need is the courage to allow it to develop.

For every talent there are at least a dozen ways of turning it into a career and earning a living – and not just a mediocre living, but a very successful one that allows you to have all those good things in life that you believe you have a right to.

You can change direction at any time in your life, the only thing that prevents you is your own belief in your limitations. You may have to go without for a while, live on a reduced income or, cope with the disapproval of the family, but still you can stop what you are doing and follow your heart's desire.

To begin to see how you could take your talents and turn them into your success, you need first to identify them. Off the top of your head, name them: things you do easily, things you enjoy, things that are free from pressure, guilt, or doubt, things you do naturally well.

Did you do this? It should have been spontaneous, without having to ponder the answers or question and abandon the thoughts that came to mind.

From experience of doing this exercise with people, I know that many of you will have discarded some thoughts as being of no value when it comes to using them to become successful. Some of you will have felt that you have no talents at all.

Can you talk easily to people? Then perhaps you didn't know that a professional speaker can earn up to £5,000 in one evening! Yes, that is a talent and can be used in a hundred different ways. It can be channelled into teaching, the theatre, counselling, local council, parliament, and so on.

If you find it easy to be meticulously tidy and are patient, you could have a successful career in chemistry or research.

Perhaps you are good at following a fitness programme – you believe in a healthy diet and self-discipline; you find it easy to train every day, get up early and run ten miles before breakfast. Could you start a Healthy Mind/Healthy Body gymnasium? People pay thousands of pounds to health clubs because they lack the motivation and discipline to follow a programme for themselves.

Yes, you may argue, but there are already hundreds of people doing these kinds of jobs so why should I be more successful than the rest? Why should I be the one to command a higher income? Because you are doing something that they are not. You have put together the essential ingredients: tenacity, a belief in yourself and your right to success, total dedication, and joy in doing what you naturally do well. You are also uninhibited by what other people think of you – you are free to control your own destiny.

Now you begin to look for obstacles. Stop! Look for the positives. Look for how you *could* make it work. It is absolutely true that if you think you can't, you won't.

You say that to reach your goal you need capital, but you have none. How then could you raise some? Who do you know that would have enough belief in you to invest in your dream? How do you convince them? Do your sums well. Be realistic. Keep your feet firmly on the ground and then . . . you fire them with your enthusiasm. There is still plenty of money around and it has to be invested in something. A friend, colleague or relative may support you simply because they believe in you. The banks will want more than this – you will have to sell them the idea.

Usually, if you want to do something that requires initial capital and you have to provide some of it (your demonstration of believing in yourself), then you may have to keep on your existing job, take on an extra one and save, save, save. Did you ever want something desperately as a child and the only way to get it was to go without sweets and save your pocket money? And did you save up and get that thing? If you could exercise such self-discipline then, you can do it now. The principle is the same.

Indulge for a few minutes in a dream. Allow yourself to experience what it feels like to be one hundred percent successful in whatever way you see personal success . . .

Was it one of the greatest feelings you ever had? It needs to be if you aim to get there. It has to be worth it to you.

Now go back to your talents. This time I'm going to ask you to choose two that stand out above all the rest – two that you feel comfortable and sure about. These are the ones you can confidently use as the foundation for your success. What do you really enjoy doing that comes naturally to you? Make a list of ways in which you could use or express these two talents. You may find you need only one.

Let me share with you how this came about for me (top of my list came natural motivation followed by compassion).

In the following ten years I built a successful practice as a consultant hypnotherapist and psychotherapist – work I thoroughly enjoyed doing. I certainly needed motivation for there was no one with whom I could confer or who could direct me to further studies or training, and if caring hadn't come naturally to me I would have found it impossible to listen to other people's problems hour after hour. I was then invited to lecture on using the unconscious mind – something else I enjoyed – which brought me into contact with a lot more people and I was able to continue to develop my ideas and skills. It is a wonderful truth that as you use your talents, more are uncovered and your world expands.

Then came my next goal. I had, all my life, enjoyed writing. Over the years a number of my short stories and articles had been accepted for publication, but my family commitments prevented me from having the continuity of time to write a full-length book. Finally the family grew up and left home and I was free to write without too many interruptions. I wrote a book, and then another, and another. I could not find a publisher who would risk an unknown writer. I believed in what I had written but seemed to have come up against a brick wall. There was only one thing to do – I had to publish myself. I knew absolutely nothing about publishing, but I believed people would enjoy my writing and that it could help them – much of what I wrote had been learned through my work and experiences over the preceding ten years. The next eight months I saved until I could pay a company to print the book for me. While this was happening I utilized the time learning how to use a computer so that I could produce what is known as camera-ready copy – this makes the costs considerably less.

The book sold sufficiently well for me to produce my second one. I began to be noticed. A local publisher asked for first refusal on my next book – they have just published the first in a series of stories I wrote to help children with problems. They also agreed to publish another book helping abused children.

Not a Jeffrey Archer yet, but I'm getting there! When I'm sufficiently successful I will aim to get one of my books filmed for television. I hope you enjoy watching it!

Don't be fooled by the media – a personality does not always spell success. Often someone is selected and hyped up because that is what makes money – it does not necessarily mean that the 'personality' has succeeded in what he or she set out to do.

The following tips can help you along the way.

- Make your goal the subject you choose, not the monetary gain.

- Give yourself mini-goals along the way.

- Listen to other people but make your own decisions.

- Keep yourself grounded – don't allow yourself to be swept along by a situation.

- Dare to say *No*.

- Move forward with confidence, but cautiously.

- Spend wisely. (Many a business has gone wrong because the directors began to order expensive cars, to eat and dine at the most exclusive places, and to buy or rent premises which were beyond their means.) People are more impressed by the goods you produce or the service you provide than how big a car or house you own.

- Keep your goal in front of you at all times – it is your motivator.

To know whether you have rightly chosen to use your talents in a specific way, you need to discover what sort of a person you are. This will help you direct your skills and ability into the best areas to ensure your success.

Most of the time we see ourselves through other people's eyes – the way in which we reflect off them is what we think we are. And we all put on different faces in different situations. So which one is the real you?

When you totally lose awareness of self you are most able to be yourself. It's a bit like getting glimpses of yourself when you are not watching. How are you when you are teaching a small child to read? What sort of a person are you when you are writing a letter to a friend? Who is that person cooking dinner? What sort of person is it digging in the garden or designing a new flower-bed?

At these moments, when you have no need to present an image to the world, how are you? Do you like what you perceive? Is this person patient, caring, confident? Does this person give up easily? Does this person have ideas and does he or she carry them through? You are taking a look at yourself from the outside and what you discover will tell you whether you have the ability to follow through and become successful. If it feels right with you it is almost certainly right for you.

Who is Everyone?

We often limit ourselves with generalizations.

Everyone says I shouldn't do it – does this mean the whole world, people who really know what is best and right for you, or your immediate family and friends? You may have a desire to push off and explore a certain country for six months but the family are scared on your behalf as it is an unknown – they try to dissuade you. They don't know what is good for you but they allow their fear of losing you to be transmitted. It may feel as if *everyone* is saying don't, but if you move away from those who are emotionally involved with you (or even envious of your opportunity or adventurous spirit) you could get a very different picture.

They say it's best I don't leave home yet – again, ask yourself who *they* are, and what is their intention in discouraging you?

Nobody in their right senses believes . . . so if you do you're crazy? Of course you have the right to question and the intelligence to take heed of other folk's advice and opinions, but you then make your own decisions.

*We **all** knew it wouldn't work* – how many times has a relationship floundered because of this negative attitude by friends and family. Sometimes you have to follow your heart no matter what anyone says. Having a go at running your own business is, to a certain extent, a gamble. If it wasn't, there would be many more having a try. You may not make it first time, but you will have gained experience in a way that is of far more value than accepting that other people's opinions are always right. Don't allow the pressure of the masses to prevent you from daring to be different and to succeed.

The *everyone* syndrome loses its power over you when you stop and ask yourself just *who is everyone and why are they trying to influence me*? The measure of your success lies in how you value your own worth.

18

Letting Go

I considered for some time whether to put this chapter at the beginning or at the end of the book. Finally I decided that it was really a summary of everything else I had written – if you don't let go you can't ever change. Daring to be, means letting go of any inhibitions or beliefs that have been restricting your life.

In order to dare, you have to change, and you cannot change without letting go of old habits, preconceived ideas, and any thoughts that the things I suggest may be fine for someone else but are not for you. The ideas, suggestions and exercises contained in this book are for anyone who dares to change – *they are for you*.

Please take the time here to do the following visualization. Imagine that you are walking along a cliff path. Suddenly the ground beneath your feet begins to crumble. You drop to your knees. Sixty feet below the sea is pounding the rocks. The ground is still crumbling. Frantically, you dig your fingers into the turf. You find some rock buried beneath the surface and press your palms against it. The lower part of your body and legs are now suspended over the crashing waves. Desperately you hold on, but the ground is still crumbling and you cannot scramble back.

The muscles in your arms begin to ache, red hot pains run up and down your spine, your head is spinning, *but you dare not let go.*

Suddenly someone calls out to you. 'Let go. It's okay, just let yourself fall.'

'I can't,' you yell back. 'There's a 60-foot drop.'

'There's also a ledge just below your feet. I'm standing on it. Let go, I'm right here.'

Peering anxiously over your shoulder you see the head and shoulders of someone beneath you. It's true. You really can let go.

With an overwhelming sense of relief, you unwind your fingers from the soil and rock and feel your body drop a few feet. There is a little jolt to your body and you land on firm ground. It is probably the most wonderful moment of your whole life.

'It's okay! Just let go.'

'Now we have to get down,' the rescuer says. 'Lucky I was fossil hunting and saw you. Follow me.'

It still isn't easy, there are a number of obstacles to overcome, but you know you'll make it. After hanging on, this seems easy in comparison. Twenty minutes later you are walking on the beach watching the waves gently lapping the shore. You have never felt so good in your whole life.

Only a story – and yet this is exactly what happens when you decide to let go. Hanging on to the old way, to past illusions, to bad experiences, is far harder and much more frightening than letting go. When you finally use your courage and let go, you will wonder why on earth you struggled to hang on for so long. Letting go is a most elevating feeling.

There is nothing to hold you back from making your own way in life and your own decisions. The only things holding you back are the fears you create in your mind. When you finally let go you will discover new opportunities, new friends, a whole new world of awareness.

You will realize that you don't have to feel bad about yourself or anything you do. You can take obstacles and turn them into challenges; failures will become learning experiences; people are no longer to be feared; you will see that what other people think or say is, after all, only their opinion.

It is impossible to move into the future while you are holding the door shut. Once you let go, you can push open doors and choose which ones you want to pass through.

Many times we cause our own suffering and carry heavy burdens of guilt, believing that by so doing the pain will buy us atonement for our sins or misdeeds. We see it, either consciously or unconsciously, as a kind of bargain with God. This achieves nothing except to make ourselves and others miserable. Self-punishment is a waste of life. Self-condemnation and self-judgment are destructive and only result in negativity. What we do need to do is to take the experience and make something good out of it.

If we believe that we have committed some crime, we carry around the resulting guilt like a heavy burden. It achieves nothing and yet we believe we have to carry this with us – sometimes for life! If someone has died and you burden yourself with guilt, you prevent yourself from ever going forward and making something worthwhile out of the years you have left. Letting go of guilt and doing something positive makes so much more sense.

Talking over misdeeds, and from this gaining a better understanding of yourself, should lead to a higher level of life. It should lead to healing, but if you find yourself recounting your story over and over again without any sense of feeling better about things, it is a signal that you need to let go.

Guilt is self-imposed, no one and nothing makes you feel guilty, only the way you view yourself.

Often we only have the courage to let go when there seems no alternative. We hold on stubbornly to situations that are doing us no good at all until something forces us to admit we are wrong, or that something won't work.

Do you know people who repeatedly tell stories of woe? Not only do they embellish these, building them up out of all proportion, but they begin to glory in them. This gives them identity, making them feel important.

An old lady I went to visit told me sadly that no one came to see her anymore. I spoke to her family about this. 'When we visit her she spends the whole time telling us how awful her life has been,' they said. 'We can't bear it any longer.'

I counsel people who have repeated their story so many times that they don't know how to stop the record. They don't want to listen or to accept that there is any other way for them. They are chained by their own thoughts to the past. This becomes a way of life, even their reason for living. They go on and on punishing themselves by re-counting how badly they were treated as a child, or how heartless their partner turned out to be, or how irritable and unkind they were to a parent who is now dead. It gives them an identity, albeit a negative one. There is nothing I can do to help, although they tell me that is what they seek.

Josie was such a person. She told me she was constantly in pain and had too many things wrong with her to even begin to list them. Her pain had all started, she told me, when her son left home and married a most unsuitable girl. When I asked Josie to tell me specifically where she experienced the pain, she told me it was everywhere.

'Is it in your nose?' I asked.

'Yes,' she said.

I tried again: 'Is it in your scalp?'

She nodded. 'It is all over my body.'

She couldn't allow herself to admit to the tiniest bit of her not suffering, and I knew she had repeated this story many times.

Of course it can happen very differently. When I met Ed he had suffered for over ten years with very severe pains in his legs. Sometimes they would disappear for months and then, just as mysteriously, they would return. After a time Ed was able to recognize that the pain coincided with when he was about to attempt something where there was a possibility of failure. The pain prevented him from pursuing that thing and he therefore avoided the anticip-ated failure.

Months later I was asked to visit him in hospital. I found him in such pain that he had seriously considered suicide. The medical staff had found no drug that eased the pain and he was quite desperate.

I asked Ed to start with his toes and identify exactly where he was experiencing the pain. He realized there wasn't actually any pain in his toes – or his feet. We progressed steadily, examining the feelings in his ankles, calf muscles, knees, thigh muscles. Suddenly Ed realized what was happening. He told me: 'I have no pain anywhere. I was in a state of hysteria. I was so afraid of it coming back that I was afraid to let it go'.

This is where Ed's healing began.

If you find yourself hanging on to your tale of suffering, ill-treatment, being misunderstood or persecuted, ask yourself what's behind it. Why do you need to hold on? What do you gain? Are you doing it for sympathy, to get attention? Do you need to hide behind it? Have you a need to convince people you are a victim?

Most of us from time to time could confess to hanging on to a tale of woe in this way. Usually something happens to drag us out of it. You may have been telling people for some time how lousy men are and how you'll never trust one again – and then along comes a really nice guy who makes you feel precious and loved and you are only too happy to let go of that old story.

Sometimes people want to hold on to their problem more than they want to find a way out.

Letting go also means letting go of those we believe need our support or control. To enjoy life to the full, we need to be able to stand alone. The other person, or persons, we have leaned upon may not always be around. How can we ever hope to express ourselves freely while we continually depend on another? In marriage, both husband and wife need to be able to stand alone. Where this does not happen, the burden and dependence of one upon the other prevents personal development and growth.

I knew a woman who had no opinions of her own. She turned to her husband before ever replying – even to the simplest question or request. Over the years this dependence (which he had cultivated) had completely destroyed her confidence. She had never even been shopping without him. She did not know how to make choices. She had nothing of herself to give. She had lost her identity. I wondered what would happen if he were to die first, or to leave her.

Kevin was 32 when I met him. He found relationships with women very difficult. Whenever there was any indication that a friendship might develop into something deeper he panicked and backed off.

One day he talked to me of his mother. He was her youngest son and she doted on him. Although he had moved away from home and bought himself a house in an endeavour to become independent, she still visited him several times a week, cleaning and doing his washing.

'She has done everything for me,' he said. 'She has ruined my life.' Here was a mother who could never let go.

Back to loving – dole out a little compassion and understanding to yourself. Where you experience bad feelings about past deeds remember that you did your best at the time. It is only because you have moved forward and developed a new awareness that you can see now how you might have done things differently but, given the pressures, the circumstances, and the mental and emotional state you were in at that time, you did your best.

Holding on to old ways and beliefs may make you feel safe, but will never allow you to attain a higher level of being.

It is not the misdeed, sin or loss that we carry around with us that hurts, but our thoughts about it. We do not have to pay for something we did in the past, neither must we expect payment from other people. By thinking in this way we only continue to carry around the pain.

Bitterness and resentment achieve nothing, but when you let go and freely forgive yourself – and others – you will feel so much better. You cannot feel at rights with the world or become whole when such negative thoughts are gnawing away at you. You cannot let go until you forgive.

Living in the past and repeating to yourself, or to anyone who will listen, the dreadful things you believe have been done or said against you, prevents you from living in the present. You miss what is going on and opportunities are lost. Your history is not your destiny, you can choose to change.

Holding on to your defences is like building a brick wall: your very behaviour separates you from others and prevents growth. How often have you felt compelled to prove someone wrong, make them take back what they said, protect your reputation? If you still have those feelings you are controlled by other people. You are better off disconnected from anyone who is influenced and persuaded by the opinions or words of another concerning you. Choose friends whose opinions you value. Rest assured, you will be judged by your own actions, by those whose opinions are of real value to you.

It is almost impossible to enjoy the opening of a rose, the chuckle of a baby, or the dawn chorus, while your mind is stuck in resentment, feelings of injustice, or self-punishment.

We tell of an injustice at work, or school, or at the grocery store. People listen, they are sympathetic. It feels nice to be the centre of attention. We pile on the agony. Someone else arrives home, or in the office, and we tell the story again. Soon it seems impossible to stop talking about it; we drive the nail in deeper until it becomes part of us. We fail to notice that people have become bored and don't want to listen any more – they have certainly stopped showing sympathy.

Have you had an experience like that? Has someone caused you to suffer a hardship or indignity that you are not prepared to let go?

Often we want to hurt because we are hurting. Forgiveness removes the pain far more effectively than revenge. You only have to look at a family reunion after there has been a breakdown – the love and tears wash away all the heartache.

A daughter leaving home and refusing to speak to her mother because she has voiced disapproval of a boyfriend can lead to months or even years with no communication. What is missed in these situations is that when angry opinions are voiced, it doesn't mean that people have stopped loving each other.

To make someone else responsible for the way you feel means that you have given them all the power – it prevents you from overcoming that obstacle or moving forward.

Exercise Fourteen – Letting Go of Destructive Feelings

If you have any old feelings of resentment, bitterness or anger that you keep reviving or going over in your mind, now is the time to deal with them.

1 Close your eyes, breathe deeply and relax. Picture yourself sitting in front of a child's blackboard and easel. Take a piece of chalk and write down any feelings of resentment, injustice, bitterness, anger – or something you feel you can't forgive. Do you still want to hold on to that feeling? Ask yourself, *What does it achieve?* Is it holding you back from being the best kind of person you are capable of being? Are those feelings spoiling your quality of life?

2 Having decided that it is not achieving anything that is really important to you, then you are ready to let go of that feeling. Take an eraser and rub out the writing. Clear the board. Now take a deep, deep breath and let go.

3 Observe how you feel. Relieved that it's over? Loved again? Free? Spend a few minutes thinking about how good it is without those negative feelings.

4 Now write on the board any positive feelings that come to you. Make up your mind to build your life based on positive emotions.

Note: You may find you actually need to speak to the person, or persons, involved in your negative feelings at a conscious level. You may simply need to let go in your mind.

Daring to be yourself – different, successful, creative – means that you have to let go of the thoughts that are preventing you. There is no other way.

Loving yourself, and believing you have the right, enables you to express yourself in any way you want. If it is positive and for good, it will work for you. Should you attempt anything that is harmful to another you must expect to suffer the repercussions. Cause and effect is one of the laws of the universe.

To be yourself, aim for the best. Refuse to settle for less. Let go of all your old fears and conditioning and stop worrying about other people's opinions. You will reap the benefits a thousandfold.

To be successful, remember that you have as much talent and ability as any other human being. Let go of fear and go all out for what you want to achieve.

Daring to be different allows your individuality to flourish. If some people didn't dare, our world of art, design, fashion, invention, language, and the fight for equality – would stagnate and die.

Daring to love and express love enriches not only you but all those whose lives touch yours. Love is a powerful energy – there is nothing it cannot change.

Daring to stop supporting others in their illusions allows them the opportunity to grow into a new awareness.

It also gives you a new sense of self-respect.

Daring to be adventurous makes you come alive – it could change your whole life.

Daring to stay young is not laughable, it is plain commonsense. Refuse to accept the conventional image of the elderly – live life *your* way.

Dare to be happy and learn to enjoy 'now'.

Dare to commit yourself and experience a new confidence.

Dare to tell the truth – and walk away with your integrity intact.

Dare to become whole.

Further Reading

Bramson, Robert M and Harrison, Allen F, *The Art of Thinking*, Berkley Books, New York

Cleese, John and Skynner, Robin, *Families and How to Survive Them*, Mandarin, 1993

Cleese, John and Skynner, Robin, *Life and How to Survive It*, Mandarin, 1994

Dantes, Ligia, *Your Fantasies May Be Hazardous to Your Health*, Element Books, 1996

Field, Lynda, *The Self-Esteem Workbook*, Element Books, 1995

Frankl, Victor, *Man's Search for Meaning*, Hodder, 1994

Godefroy, Christian H and Steevens, D R, *Mind Power*, Piatkus, 1993

Grant, Wendy, *Are You in Control?* Element Books, 1996

Grant, Wendy, *How to be Lucky*, Eastbrook Publishing, 1994

Grant, Wendy, *You and Your Dreams*, Eastbrook Publishing, 1995

Gawain, Shakti, *Meditations*, New World Library, 1991

Hauck, Dr Paul, *How to Be Your Own Best Friend*, Sheldon Press, 1988

Meares, Ainslie, *Wealth Within*, The Hill of Content Publishing Company, 1994

Osho, *What Is Meditation?* Element Books, 1995

Roet, Dr Brian, *All in the Mind*, Optima, 1994

Sheehan, Elaine, *Health Essentials: Self-Hypnosis*, Element Books, 1995

Zukav, Gary, *The Seat of the Soul*, Century, 1991

Index